Bible Study Guide

Genesis

Good Questions Have
Small Groups Talking

By Josh Hunt

© Copyright 2015 Josh Hunt
If you enjoy this, you might check out the hundreds of lessons available at a low subscription price at
http://mybiblestudylessons.com/

All scripture quotations, unless otherwise indicated, are taken from the Holy Bible, New International Version®, NIV®. Copyright ©1973, 1978, 1984, 2011 by Biblica, Inc.™ Used by permission of Zondervan. All rights reserved worldwide. www.zondervan.com The "NIV" and "New International Version" are trademarks registered in the United States Patent and Trademark Office by Biblica, Inc.™

Contents

Genesis, Lesson #1 1

Genesis, Lesson #2 15

Genesis, Lesson #3 27

Genesis, Lesson #4 43

Genesis, Lesson #5 58

Genesis, Lesson #6 73

Genesis, Lesson #7 88

Genesis, Lesson #8 104

Genesis, Lesson #9 118

Genesis, Lesson #10 133

Genesis, Lesson #11 148

Genesis, Lesson #12 167

Genesis, Lesson #13 183

Genesis, Lesson #1
Good Questions Have Small Groups Talking
www.joshhunt.com

Email your people and challenge your people to read up on creation. Alternatively, you might invite them to watch some YouTube videos. Do a search for "creation, Genesis." Here is one cool video: https://www.youtube.com/watch?v=PtpTk2ENq7o

Genesis 1 – 2.4

OPEN

Let's each your name and one thing you love about creation—a favorite national park, or, pastime to do outdoors.

DIG

1. **Introduction. Does this account of creation agree with science?**

    Lots of people get hung up on verse 1 of chapter 1. And this presents a problem, for if one doesn't agree with the opening statement of the first sentence, it will be difficult for him to accept what follows.

    "You don't really believe that God created heaven and earth in six days, do you?" scoffs the cynic. "That might be a nice legend, even a practical parable—but you can't really take this seriously. It's just not scientific!"

Gang, the book in your hand doesn't claim to be a book of science. Yet whenever it touches on issues of science, it is absolutely infallible. There is no proven scientific fact that contradicts a single statement written in the pages of this book.

> Have ye not known? have ye not heard? hath it not been told you from the beginning? have ye not understood from the foundations of the earth? It is he that sitteth upon the circle of the earth... Isaiah 40:21, 22

Every culture, every nation, every people throughout world history believed the earth to be flat as a pancake—until Christopher Columbus proved the validity of Isaiah's words.

> He stretcheth out the north over the empty place, and hangeth the earth upon nothing. Job 26:7

God hangs the earth on nothing?

Learned scholars in India would have said, "We all know the world is held up on the backs of giant elephants." The Greeks maintained that the earth was held in place by the bulging biceps and massive shoulders of Atlas. South Sea islanders believed the earth was supported on the backs of giant tortoises.

Sure enough, the more we learn, the more we find the Bible is right all along. I like that!

"Wait a minute," some say. "Genesis 1:1 may address spirituality and theology, but it can't be taken literally—not in this day, when the theory of evolution has been accepted so completely."

Keep in mind that evolution at best is a theory—and a bankrupt one at that. Many men of science who are neither believers in Jesus Christ nor students of the Bible have turned away from the evolutionary hypothesis because it violates the most foundational, fundamental principles and laws of known science. For example, one of the most important laws of science is the Second Law of Thermodynamics. It's not a theory, not a hypothesis, but a basic principle which says everything goes from order to disorder.

If I create the outline of a horse by arranging marbles on a sheet of plywood, place my finished work in the backseat of my VW, drive around town for half an hour, when I stop the car, will the horse be more intricate? Will the horse become even finer in detail, more elaborate artistically? Or will there be a bunch of marbles on the floor?

One of the principles upon which science is predicated is the fact that everything goes from order to disorder. The theory of evolution completely violates this understanding, maintaining as it does, that things go from disorder to greater order, from simplicity to complexity.

"But the great minds embrace the theory of evolution," some insist. Do they?

> The man Discover Magazine rated as the greatest scientific thinker in history is Sir Isaac Newton. Newton was mocked because his contemporaries couldn't understand why he believed there really was a God who created the world in six days. One day, Sir Isaac made an elaborate model of the solar system, which took up the entire front room of his house. Impressed by its details, his colleagues asked him where he got the model.
>
> "I didn't get it," Newton said.
>
> "Oh. You made it?"
>
> "No, I didn't buy it. I didn't make it. No one put it here. It just appeared."
>
> And suddenly they got his point.
>
> The heavens declare the glory of God; and the firmament sheweth his handywork. Day unto day uttereth speech, and night unto night sheweth knowledge. There is no

speech nor language, where their voice is not heard. Psalm 19:1–3

The grandeur of the universe undeniably points to the existence of a Creator. But men suppress this truth, not wanting to be accountable to this Creator (Romans 1). That is why you can defend the Genesis account on the basis of science until you're blue in the face—and still fail to convince the skeptic. — Jon Courson, *Jon Courson's Application Commentary: Volume One: Genesis–Job* (Nashville, TN: Thomas Nelson, 2005), 1–2.

2. **Overview. Let's make a list on the board. What was created on each of the six days?**

   INTRODUCTION: As the final brush stroke on the canvas of God's creation, Adam and Eve were drawn into the picture as the recipients of all that had been previously made. Everything in Genesis 1:1–26 was designed for the ones created in verse 27, whom God made in His own image. As heirs of those blessings, we, too, can thank God for:

   1. This Planet, So Perfectly Designed to Meet Our Needs (vv. 1–2).

   2. The Light, Which Makes Vision Possible (vv. 3–5).

   3. The Sky, Beautiful, Full of Life-Sustaining Elements (vv. 6–8).

   4. The Soil, Perfectly Designed as Earth's Flooring (vv. 9–10).

   5. The Oceans, Awe-Inspiring, Beautiful, Teeming with Life, and Fun (v. 11).

   6. The Vegetation, from Tiny Wildflowers to Towering Redwoods (vv. 12–13).

   7. The Celestial Heavens: Sun, Moon, and Stars (vv. 13–19).

   8. The Animal Life, Strange, Odd, Fully, Frightening, and Companionable (vv. 20–25).

Robert J. Morgan, *Nelson's Annual Preacher's Sourcebook, 2007 Edition* (Nashville, TN: Thomas Nelson Publishers, 2007), 359.

3. If the sun was created on the fourth day, what was the light created on the first?

Bucaille affirms, "it is illogical, however, to mention the result (light) on the first day, when the cause of this light [the sun] was created three days later."

But almost anyone with an even elementary knowledge of science and the Bible can answer this objection. For the sun is not the only source of light in the universe. Further, it is not necessary to understand the text as saying the sun was created on the fourth day. It may have been only made to appear on the fourth day, after the mist of water vapor had cleared away so that its outline became visible. Before this its light may have been shining through, just as it does on a misty day, without observers on earth being able to see the outline of the sun. — Norman L. Geisler and Abdul Saleeb, *Answering Islam: The Crescent in Light of the Cross, 2nd ed.* (Grand Rapids, MI: Baker Books, 2002), 221–222.

4. Verses 1, 2. What do we learn about God from these verses? How is He different from us?

"In the beginning God …" God is the first-named subject in the book of Genesis, and that's appropriate. The universe in which we live had a beginning. Prior to that starting point, there was no universe. There was no up and no down, no here and no there. Just nothing—except God. He always was. Before creation God alone existed. The Hebrew word translated God has been identified as coming from a verb meaning "to fear." The God who existed from all eternity and who at one point created time and space is awesome and deserves to be held in reverence by his creatures. Everything exists for his sake, including the human race. You and I do not exist of ourselves or for ourselves. We have a right to exist only as we remain in harmony with the majestic Creator and his plan for us.

We humans have birthdays and deathdays, beginnings and endings; God has neither. He alone is eternal; nobody and nothing else is eternal. There was no bubble of gas, no cosmic dust that could have kindled the germ of life. The earliest forms of life did not originate in a blob of slime on some prehistoric pond. The elements, the materials from which our universe is made up, are not eternal. They came into existence only when God so ordered. The word order of this first sentence of the Bible seems perfectly normal in English, but Hebrew sentences normally begin with the verb. Here the word order is inverted, for the sake of emphasis. Moses wants to emphasize that there was a point of absolute beginning, when only God was in existence. — John C. Jeske, *Genesis, 2nd ed., The People's Bible* (Milwaukee, WI: Northwestern Pub. House, 2001), 10–11.

5. What do we learn about God's creation from these verses?

"God created the heavens and the earth." The Hebrew verb translated created is a very special one. In the Bible that verb (1) is used only of God's activity and (2) always expresses the origin of something extraordinary, absolutely unique. Sometimes God creates by using existing material; when he created Adam, for example, he used the dust of the ground. But if the activity described in this opening verse took place at the beginning, when only God existed, it must have been a creation out of nothing. — John C. Jeske, *Genesis, 2nd ed., The People's Bible* (Milwaukee, WI: Northwestern Pub. House, 2001), 11.

6. How does God create differently than how we create things?

A group of scientists decided that human beings had come a long way and no longer needed God. They picked one scientist to go and tell God that they did not need him anymore. The scientist went to him and said, "God, we can make it on our own. We know how life started. We know the secret. We know how to clone it. We know how to duplicate it. We can do it without you."

God listened patiently and said, "All right. What do you say we have a man-making contest?"

The scientist said, "Okay, great. We'll do it."

God said, "Now we're going to do it just the way I did back in the old days with Adam."

The scientist said, "Sure, no problem." He reached down and grabbed a handful of dirt, and God said, "No, no, no. You go get your own dirt."

That's the trick.

Talking about something that changes into something else and how long it takes for something to change into something else — that's not what most cries out for explanation. The trick is how do you get from nothing to something, and why is there something? We all want to know. — John Ortberg, *Know Doubt: Embracing Uncertainty in Your Faith* (Grand Rapids, MI: Zondervan, 2014).

7. Verses 3 – 5. Why do you think God created the light first?

We are drawn to God's radiant light. It is a light that exposes all of our spiritual and moral deficiencies, but it is not only there to reveal our shortcomings. It is also there to light the way to our salvation. God's light is there so we can see our way through the darkness and come into his light. — Greg Laurie, *Walking with Jesus: Daily Inspiration from the Gospel of John* (Grand Rapids, MI: Baker, 2007).

8. We always want to read the Bible for application. What is the application to us for the creation of light?

The sun is one aspect of God's creation that we often take for granted. After all, the sun is there each morning. It is often hot and occasionally a nuisance. Most of us spend most (if not all) of our time indoors, and the sun has become somewhat scary in our consciousness. But the truth is, healthy sun exposure can help to lift our mood and can give us more energy. Healthy interaction with the sun can really help us on this weight-management journey.

We are told that the first moment of God's creation was light. God created the sun, giving us a wonderful gift that is beautiful, and that offers joy and health (when used correctly). There are many of us who get so busy with our lives that we forget to step out into the sun. We don't give our bodies the gift of safely enjoying the light and warmth that are products of this first gift of God's creation. The truly amazing thing is, if we do enjoy God's creation responsibly, we will also be healthier. — Scott Morris, *Church Health Center, and The Church Health Center Scott Morris, 40 Days to Better Living--Weight Management* (Uhrichsville, OH: Barbour, 2013).

9. Verses 6 – 9. What exactly did God create on the second day?

On the second day (1:6–8) God separated the atmospheric waters from the terrestrial waters by an arching expanse or "space" that God called "sky." This may suggest that previously there had been a dense moisture covering the earth. By making this area of atmospheric pressure, God was making further divisions and distinctions within his creation. First light as opposed to darkness, and now water and air as opposed to dense moisture over the whole planet—conditions were beginning to come about that would support life. So God gave the command, and it happened. The report in the text is that "that is what happened." The expression in Hebrew ("and it was so") has a stronger connotation: What God created took its fixed place in time and space and was made perfect in conjunction with all other aspects of creation. — Allen Ross and John N. Oswalt, *Cornerstone Biblical Commentary: Genesis, Exodus, vol. 1* (Carol Stream, IL: Tyndale House Publishers, 2008), 38.

10. Verse 9ff. What did God create on the third day?

God gathered the waters and caused the dry land to appear, thus making "earth" and "seas." Israel's pagan neighbors believed all kinds of myths about the heavens, the earth, and the seas; but Moses made it clear that Elohim, the one true God, was Lord of them all. For the first time, God said that what He had done was "good" (v. 10). God's creation is still good, even though it travails because of sin (Rom. 8:20–22) and has been ravaged and exploited by sinful people.

God also caused plant life to appear on the earth: the grasses, the seed-producing herbs, and the fruit-bearing trees. God decreed that each would reproduce "after its kind," which helps to make possible order in nature. God has set reproductive limits for both plants and animals (Gen. 1:21) because He is the Lord of Creation. There's no suggestion here of any kind of "evolution." God was preparing the earth for a habitation for humans and for animals, and the plants would help to provide their food. A second time, God said that His work was good (v. 12). — Warren W. Wiersbe, *Be Basic, "Be" Commentary Series* (Colorado Springs, CO: Chariot Victor Pub., 1998), 26–27.

11. God already created the light. What did He create on the fourth day?

On the fourth day, God made the sun and the moon.

Jesus is the Light of the world (John 8:12). He said we are also to be lights (Matthew 5:14). He is the greater light—the sun. We are the lesser light—the moon—reflecting His light to our dark world.

I recently watched the moon appear smaller and smaller in an eclipse, and was reminded that to whatever extent the world gets between the sun and the moon is the extent to which the light of the sun upon the moon is diminished. The same thing is true with me and you. Jesus is the sun; we're the moon; and to whatever degree we allow the world to come between us, His light in our lives will fade proportionately. If you were to chart your own life tonight, would you be a full moon, a three-quarter moon, half moon, quarter moon, or eclipsed moon? It all depends on how much of the world you allow to creep in between you and the Son. — Jon Courson,

*Jon Courson's Application Commentary: Volume One: Genesis–Job (*Nashville, TN: Thomas Nelson, 2005), 4.

12. Verse 20. How many things did God create on this day?

Science has described around 2 million species but it is estimated that there could be between 5 to 100 million different species on Earth. This incredible biodiversity is what enriches our lives on this planet and is also essential for our survival. http://wwf.panda.org/about_our_earth/species/

13. What are some of your favorite animals?

But there's something more. Ellen Davis writes that God's questions are indicating something about the kind of person he is. They are filled with references to God's extravagant goodness and provision even though there is no "strategic gain" in it at all.

"Who cuts a channel for the torrents of rain, . . .

to water a land where no man lives, a desert with no one in it,

to satisfy a desolate wasteland and make it sprout with grass?"

These lines would jump out at the reader in Job's day. Life in Israel depended on rainfall. They would never waste water. So why would God water "a land where no one lives"?

Because God is a God of gratuitous goodness. And he is uncontrollably generous. He is irrationally loving. He is good for no reason at all. He is good just because he loves to give. He sends streams of living water flowing out of sheer exuberant generosity. There is a wilderness where no one lives, yet it is full of beauty and grace because God makes a river run through it.

God delights in animals that are of no apparent use at all. The ostrich looks goofy and flaps her wings "joyfully" as if they could get her somewhere. She lays eggs and can't even remember where she left the babies. She doesn't seem to be worth much of an investment. But when she runs—oh my! "She laughs at horse and rider." Why would God waste such talent?

"I made the behemoth," God says—probably the hippopotamus. The creature is of no particular use: "Can anyone capture him when he is on the watch, With barbs can anyone pierce his nose?" The ancient world considered the hippo a chaotic monster that had to be destroyed—but not God. "He ranks first among the works of God."

It's as if God is saying, "Best thing I ever did. I had my 'A' game going the day I made the behemoth." God takes pleasure in wild oxen that will never plow; the wild donkey that will never be tamed; mountain goats that give birth in secret places man will never see; the leviathan that no one can catch. "Nothing on earth is his equal."

God creates, cares for, gives to, and delights in animals that don't appear to be good for anything. Why should God love a world like that? Anne Dillard writes, "Because the creator loves pizzazz." — *God Is Closer Than You Think: This Can Be the Greatest Moment of Your Life Because This Moment Is the Place Where You Can Meet God* John Ortberg.

14. What is mean by the old-earth and young-earth theories of creation? Which makes more sense to you?

Viewers of the Ken Ham and Bill Nye debate on Tuesday were left with the impression that Christians, or creationists in particular, all hold to a young earth view. The debate, however, ignored other Christian perspectives, most notably "old earth creationism" of the intelligent design movement – another Christian approach to faith and science.

"Young earth creationists believe that the world was created in six twenty-four hour days and that the earth is no more than 6,000 years old," explained Jay Richards, senior fellow at The Discovery Institute, in an interview with The Christian Post on Thursday. By contrast, "Old earth creationists try to connect the days to long geological time periods." Richards, co-author of The Privileged Planet: How Our Place in the Cosmos Is Designed for Discovery, holds to this latter view.

In the debate, Ken Ham articulated his belief in the young earth view, and attacked Christians who hold to the old earth as inconsistent. He argued against the evidence of radiometric and astrological dating – where scientists study the decay of minerals and the distance of the stars to claim that the universe is at least millions of years old. "I claim there's only one infallible dating method – a witness who was there and who knows everything and who told us – that's the Word of God," Ham, president of Answers in Genesis, said.

Ham acknowledged that old earth creationists can still be Christians "because salvation is conditioned upon faith in Christ, not the age of the earth," but he did insist they were twisting Scripture. Old earth Christians defended their view, arguing that the Bible does not require believers to believe creation took exactly six twenty-four hour days.

Read more at http://www.christianpost.com/news/creation-science-old-earth-vs-young-earth-114219/#HE3IGhGmpteсaAHI.99

15. Verse 26. What do we learn about ourselves from this verse?

Amazingly enough, research shows that the best moments of our lives don't come from leisure or pleasure. They don't involve sex or chocolate. They come when we are totally immersed in a significant task that is challenging, yet matches up well to our highest abilities. In these moments, a person is so caught up in an activity that time somehow seems to be altered; their attention is fully focused, but without having to work at it. They are deeply aware without being self-conscious; they are being stretched and challenged, but without a sense of stress or worry. They have a sense of engagement or oneness with what they are doing.

This condition is called "flow," because people experiencing it often use the metaphor of feeling swept up by something outside themselves. Studies have been done over the past thirty years with hundreds of thousands of subjects to explore this phenomenon of flow. Ironically, people experience it far more in their work than they do in their leisure. In fact, the time of week when "flow" is at its lowest ebb in America is Sunday morning, because so many people do not know what they want to do. Sitting around does not produce flow.

I believe this picture of "flow" is actually a description of what the exercise of dominion was intended to look like. God says in Genesis that human beings are to "rule" over the earth, or to exercise "dominion." We often think of these words in terms of "dominating" or "bossing around." But the true idea behind them is that we are to invest our abilities to create value on the earth, to plant and build and write and organize and heal and invent in ways that bless people and make the earth flourish. — John Ortberg, *The Me I Want to Be* (Grand Rapids, MI: Zondervan, 2010).

16. What do we learn about work from this verse?

The scholar N. T. Wright has a wonderful image of this. Picture human beings as mirrors set at a forty-five degree angle between heaven and earth. We were created to reflect God's care and dominion to the earth, and we were made to express the worship and gratitude of creation up to God. This is what we do when we work. — John Ortberg, *The Me I Want to Be* (Grand Rapids, MI: Zondervan, 2010).

17. How does God view work differently than we do?

Heaven's calendar has seven Sundays a week. God sanctifies each day. He conducts holy business at all hours and in all places. He uncommons the common by turning kitchen sinks into shrines, cafes into convents, and nine-to-five workdays into spiritual adventures.

Workdays? Yes, workdays. He ordained your work as something good. Before he gave Adam a wife or a child, even before he gave Adam britches, God gave Adam a job. "Then the LORD God took the man and put him into the garden of

Eden to cultivate it and keep it" (Gen. 2:15 NASB). Innocence, not indolence, characterized the first family. . . .

God unilaterally calls all the physically able to till the gardens he gives. God honors work. So honor God in your work.
— Max Lucado, *Grace for the Moment® Volume Ii: More Inspirational Thoughts for Each Day of the Year* (Nashville: Thomas Nelson, 2006).

18. What do we learn about God from the creation story?

A mighty hand went to work....

Out of nothing came light. Out of light came day....

Canyons were carved. Oceans were dug. Mountains erupted out of flatlands. Stars were flung. A universe sparkled.

The hand behind it was mighty.

He is mighty. — Max Lucado, *Everyday Blessings: Inspirational Thoughts from the Published Works of Max Lucado.* (Nashville, TN: Thomas Nelson, Inc., 2004).

19. What do you want to recall from today's discussion?

20. How can we support one another in prayer this week?

Genesis, Lesson #2
Good Questions Have Small Groups Talking
www.joshhunt.com

Genesis 2.4 - 25

OPEN

Let's each your name and what is your favorite animal in the zoo?

DIG

1. **Overview. How does this account of creation differ from chapter 1?**

   Genesis 1 and 2 both deal with the creation story. Chapter 1 uses a wide-angle lens to give us the big picture. Chapter 2 uses a zoom lens to deal specifically with the creation of man. — Jon Courson, *Jon Courson's Application Commentary: Volume One: Genesis–Job* (Nashville, TN: Thomas Nelson, 2005)

2. **Verse 5. What did the earth look like at this point?**

   The scene described here is that of a barren desert. There is neither shrub nor plant in the fields. Two factors account for this emptiness. God is not doing what he is accustomed to doing—sending rain. Nor is there a man to till the soil, something that he will do when he arrives on the scene. If plant life is to grow in this garden, it will be due to a joint operation. God will do his part and man will expedite his responsibilities. Rain is not sufficient. Tillage is not sufficient. God is not a tiller of the soil and man is not a sender of rain.

But the presence of one being without the other guarantees the perpetuation of desertlike conditions.

It would be premature to say that 2:5 flatly contradicts 1:11–12. The latter two verses describe the creation of vegetation on the third day, three days before man is created. In 2:5–7 the reader is informed that when God created man there were no plants or shrubs. To begin with, if this is such a blatant inconsistency, why did the redactor do nothing to smooth it out? It will do no good to say that the biblical compilers hesitated to tamper with the received texts, for the source analysis theory has already posited redactional tampering in the addition of a second name for God in the received J document. Is it logical that the editors would edit the text at one point to remove possible confusion but would leave untouched chronological inconsistencies that the reader might find puzzling and unexpected?

Indeed, one of the two words used here—ʿēśeḇ, plant—was also used in 1:11–12. The other word—śîaḥ, shrub—does not appear in ch. 1. It occurs only three more times in the OT. Young Ishmael was placed under a śîaḥ in the wilderness by his mother (21:15). A śîaḥ grows in a place where the dejected and the debilitated seek shelter and perhaps food (Job 30:4, 7). Thus the reference is to some kind of desert shrub or bush. — Victor P. Hamilton, *The Book of Genesis, Chapters 1–17, The New International Commentary on the Old Testament* (Grand Rapids, MI: Wm. B. Eerdmans Publishing Co., 1990), 153–154.

3. Verse 6. How was the garden watered?

The Lord evidently had a built-in sprinkler system on automatic timer which kept everything watered, for before the days of Noah, there was no rain on the earth, which explains why the sight of him building an ark would have seemed laughable to his contemporaries. — Jon Courson, *Jon Courson's Application Commentary: Volume One: Genesis–Job* (Nashville, TN: Thomas Nelson, 2005)

4. Verse 7. How is the creation of man different from the animals?

God's breathing "the breath of life" into the man transformed him into a living being ("living person," 2:7, NLT). "Person" represents nepesh [5315, 5883] (soul, being), which refers here to the whole person. Since both animals and humans are referred to as nepesh (cf. 1:21, 24), the translation "being" works best.

It is the way in which the man came to be a living being that distinguishes him from the animals. God breathed into his nostrils "the breath of life" (2:7). This breath (neshamah [5397, 5972]) from God made man a living spiritual being, with the capacity for spiritual understanding, discerning right from wrong, and communing with God. With this special act of creation, the reader can appreciate the significance of the Fall. When sin entered the human race, the spiritual capacities were ruined, making a re-creation essential for fellowship with God. Since the Fall, regeneration by the divine Breath, the Holy Spirit, is essential for people to be restored to the life God had intended them to have from the beginning (cf. John 20:22). — Allen Ross and John N. Oswalt, *Cornerstone Biblical Commentary: Genesis, Exodus, vol. 1* (Carol Stream, IL: Tyndale House Publishers, 2008), 43–44.

5. Verse 7. What do we learn about ourselves from this verse?

What do you see when you look in the mirror? A slightly disfigured person, far from perfect? When you evaluate your talents and gifts, do you see a sorely lacking individual? When you look into your heart, do you see someone with characteristics that turn into flaws way too quickly? Be encouraged; when God looks at you, He sees only beauty.

As sure as God's divine hands formed Adam from the dust of the earth, so has He formed you in your mother's womb. He sculpted you with depth and insight. He created your personhood—that part that makes you, you. He has placed within you very carefully chosen traits and characteristics that are unique to you alone. That person you can't stand to look at is the perfectly clad bride of the divine Bridegroom. Exalt Him for who you are: His precious child, formed by His divine hands. — Lisa Arnold, *For Sanity's Sake: Devotions for the Temporarily Insane* (Greenville, SC: Ambassador International, 2015).

6. **Verse 15. We touched on this last week. How does the Christian faith see work differently than the world?**

DO YOU BELIEVE God wants you to be joy filled?

Since you are reading this book, I am pretty sure I know how you answered that question. Here's another one: Can you imagine that God wants you to live with joy but merely tolerate what you do for a living? Do you believe God wants his children to be bored and miserable for half of their waking hours? I don't think so. Not any more than you would want your sons or daughters, week after week, to endure work that deflates and demotivates them. I have concluded that our work is part of God's plan for our joy.

Our work demands a significant portion of our lives here on the earth. God invented work because it is good for our souls. Work is not a punishment from God—in fact, it even existed before the fall of man. Genesis 2:15 says, "The LORD God took the man [Adam] and put him in the Garden of Eden to work it and take care of it" (NIV). Work is a gift from God. This mind-set is the key to gaining joy from your work, not losing joy from your work. Imagine two almost identical individuals, living almost identical lives in the same town. The only difference is that one views his work as a necessary evil and the other as her calling. Is there any way that their respective outlooks do not influence their capacity for joy?

Accept that your work is your ministry; it is a platform that God leverages to help you grow spiritually. It is also one of the most significant stewardship opportunities you will ever experience. When you commit your work to God and yourself to excellence, you gain immense pleasure and satisfaction. You only have to observe his creation to see that God loves excellence. — Tommy Newberry, *40 Days to a Joy-Filled Life: Living the 4:8 Principle* (Carol Stream, IL: Tyndale, 2012).

7. Can you think of other biblical verses that inform our understanding of work?

God made the world excellent, and he intended us for excellence as well. From Proverbs through the parables, God's Word shows he loves excellence, prudence, and productivity. Here's a sampling:

1) "In all labor there is profit, but idle chatter leads only to poverty" (Proverbs 14:23, NKJV).

2) "Whatever your hand finds to do, do it with your might" (Ecclesiastes 9:10, NKJV).

3) "Whether you eat or drink, or whatever you do, do all to the glory of God" (1 Corinthians 10:31, NKJV).

4) "Commit your actions to the LORD, and your plans will succeed" (Proverbs 16:3, NLT).

5) "Anyone who has been stealing must steal no longer, but must work, doing something useful with their own hands, that they may have something to share with those in need" (Ephesians 4:28, NIV).

6) "Lazy people take food in their hand but don't even lift it to their mouth" (Proverbs 26:15, NLT).

7) "Do you see a man who excels in his work? He will stand before kings" (Proverbs 22:29, NKJV).

8) "The plans of the diligent lead surely to plenty" (Proverbs 21:5, NKJV).

9) "Do not love sleep, lest you come to poverty" (Proverbs 20:13, NKJV).

10) "The desire of the lazy man kills him, for his hands refuse to labor" (Proverbs 21:25, NKJV).

In Scripture, excellence is both promoted and honored. Considering how much time will be absorbed in your vocation, can you think of a more vital area where your example can witness to others? Uncover the joy in your work. If you haven't already found it, it is usually just a quick attitude adjustment away. But if you can't discover it, create it. You essentially have two choices: either transition into work you love or, if this option is not immediately on the horizon, find ways to love what you currently are obliged to do.

Our work is not a secular activity but an extension of our walk with God. Unfortunately, too many believers, not to mention the rest of the population, still think of their work as a remote island, somehow isolated from their spiritual lives. Some even view work as a necessary evil, a kind of penance that must be paid so that they may better enjoy the evenings and weekends. This attitude does not glorify God, and it is not for you. — Tommy Newberry, *40 Days to a Joy-Filled Life: Living the 4:8 Principle* (Carol Stream, IL: Tyndale, 2012).

8. Verses 16, 17. Why did God create a tree that Adam and Eve could not eat?

Why would God place in the Garden a tree from which Adam and Eve were not to eat? Because God desires a loving relationship with man. And true love is built on choice. Therefore, in placing the Tree of Knowledge of Good and Evil in the Garden, God said to mankind, "If you want to kill our relationship, if you want to turn your back on Me, I must provide this opportunity. All you have to do, Adam, to end our relationship is to eat from that tree." — Jon Courson, *Jon Courson's Application Commentary: Volume One: Genesis–Job* (Nashville, TN: Thomas Nelson, 2005), 7.

9. What is the consequence of disobedience?

The Lord is so good because He made it as scary as possible. He said, "If you eat from that tree, it's going to kill you." What else could the Father have done to provide a choice, but also to say, "Don't do that."?

Notice God does not say, "If you eat of that tree, I'm going to kill you." He says, "If you eat of the tree, it will kill you." For many years, I thought that if I did something wrong, God would track me down. No, the Bible says, "Be sure your sin will find you out" (Numbers 32:23). It is sin that tracks us down, our sin that wipes us out. In the fruit of the Tree of the Knowledge of Good and Evil, perhaps there was something carcinogenic, something that would cause men to begin to die. — Jon Courson, *Jon Courson's Application Commentary: Volume One: Genesis–Job* (Nashville, TN: Thomas Nelson, 2005), 7.

10. What do we learn about this tree from Revelation 22.2?

The whole world must have been beautiful and lush before Adam and Eve's fall, but the Garden was something really special. Think of all of the gorgeous places you've ever seen—every vision of every tropical isle on every travel brochure. Eden surpassed all of those. Eden was perfection.

In the midst of this earthly paradise was the Tree of Life. We later learn that the fruit of this tree, if eaten, allowed you to live forever. That is why, after Adam and Eve ate of the Tree of the Knowledge of Good and Evil, God made sure they could not eat of the Tree of Life. The Creator would not allow Adam and Eve to live forever in their fallen state.

Interestingly enough, we're told that in the New Jerusalem we will eventually have access to this tree. Revelation 22:2 says, "In the middle of its street, and on either side of the river, was the tree of life, which bore twelve fruits, each tree yielding its fruit every month. The leaves of the tree were for the healing of the nations." — Greg Laurie, *Married. Happily.: Secrets to a Great Marriage* (Dana Point, CA: Kerygma Publishing—Allen David Books, 2011).

11. Genesis 2.18. Circle every occurrence of the phrase, "it was good." Notice this verse. What is not good?

God, who seven times has declared various aspects of creation "good," now declares that "it is not good" for Adam to be without a suitable partner (2:18). The reference to something that is "not good" sets the scene for one of the most evocative and beautiful stories in the OT. God forms the animals and birds and brings them before Adam; he gives them names, but no appropriate partner for him is found among them (2:19–20). The parade of the animals before the human would highlight their dual sexuality—male and female—and thereby accentuate the loneliness of the human being. As in the formation of Adam, God is intimately involved; he forms woman from Adam's side. A deep sleep ensures that Adam could not take credit for his partner's existence. Together they stand equal before God (2:23). Although the woman is referred to as "helper," this is not an indication of inferiority or lower status. — James McKeown, *Genesis, The Two Horizons Old Testament Commentary* (Grand Rapids, MI; Cambridge, U.K.: William B. Eerdmans Publishing Company, 2008), 33–34.

12. Verse 18. Why was it not good that Adam be alone? What bad thing happen to the lonely?

Feeling uncertain, I began to research loneliness and came across several alarming recent studies. Loneliness is not just making us sick, it is killing us. Loneliness is a serious health risk. Studies of elderly people and social isolation concluded that those without adequate social interaction were twice as likely to die prematurely.

The increased mortality risk is comparable to that from smoking. And loneliness is about twice as dangerous as obesity.

Social isolation impairs immune function and boosts inflammation, which can lead to arthritis, type II diabetes, and heart disease. Loneliness is breaking our hearts, but as a culture we rarely talk about it. http://www.slate.com/articles/health_and_science/medical_examiner/2013/08/dangers_of_loneliness_social_isolation_is_deadlier_than_obesity.html

13. Do you think our connected world has made us any less lonely?

Loneliness has doubled: 40 percent of adults in two recent surveys said they were lonely, up from 20 percent in the 1980s.

All of our Internet interactions aren't helping and may be making loneliness worse. A recent study of Facebook users found that the amount of time you spend on the social network is inversely related to how happy you feel throughout the day.

In a society that judges you based on how expansive your social networks appear, loneliness is difficult to fess up to. It feels shameful.

About a decade ago, my mom was going through a divorce from my step-father. Lonely and desperate for connection, she called a cousin she hadn't talked to in several years. On the phone, her cousin was derisive: "Don't you have any friends?"

While dealing with my own loneliness in Portland I often found myself thinking, "If I were a better person I wouldn't be lonely."

"Admitting you are lonely is like holding a big L up on your forehead," says John T. Cacioppo of the University of Chicago, who studies how loneliness and social isolation affect people's health. http://www.slate.com/articles/health_and_science/medical_examiner/2013/08/dangers_of_loneliness_social_isolation_is_deadlier_than_obesity.html

14. Verse 23. How did Adam feel when he first saw Eve?

Adam fell into a sleep, and when he awoke, there was Eve. He said, "This is now bone of my bones and flesh of my flesh." That might sound a little flat or prosaic in English, but in the original Hebrew, you can almost hear that garden rock with joy. His response was more like, "Yes! This is good! Lord, I love it!" — Greg Laurie, *Married. Happily.: Secrets to a Great*

Marriage (Dana Point, CA: Kerygma Publishing—Allen David Books, 2011).

15. What do we learn about marriage from the creation story?

I've heard many sermons (usually on Mother's Day) about "the Proverbs 31 woman." Check out that passage and you'll find a Supermom—doing the laundry, driving the kids to soccer practice, and running her own multinational corporation. No wonder her husband and children "rise up to call her blessed."

But let me give you the picture of "the Genesis 2 woman."

"Then the LORD God made a woman from the rib he had taken out of the man, and he brought her to the man" (v. 22).

I'm told that the Hebrew word for "rib" can mean "side." Clearly this woman is no minor accessory; she is a chunk of Adam, the other half of his flesh.

"The man said, 'This is now bone of my bones and flesh of my flesh; she shall be called "woman," for she was taken out of man'" (v. 23).

I'd like to think that, when he first laid eyes on this exquisite new creation, Adam said something like, "GOLLEEEEE!!!" Then when he caught his breath, he said the bone and flesh stuff. Obviously this guy is excited.

"For this reason a man will leave his father and mother and be united to his wife, and they will become one flesh" (v. 24).

Two become one; that's the story. Woman is the other half of man. We need each other. Let's stop doing battle and learn to serve. Let's discover all the blessings God has for us. Then we will truly be "couples of promise." — Kevin Leman, *Kevin, Sex Begins in the Kitchen: Creating Intimacy to Make Your Marriage Sizzle* (Grand Rapids, MI: Baker, 2006).

16. What does it mean that Eve was a helper?

From the beginning, God was clear about a woman's primary role in this world. Genesis 2:18 reads: "It is not good for the man to be alone. I will make a helper suitable for him." No one took her role as helper more seriously than Jane Hill, late wife of Los Angeles pastor E. V. Hill. She loved him deeply and devoted herself to his needs. E. V. once received a death threat from gang members indicating he would be killed the next day. He woke up the following morning "thankful to be alive," as he told it later. "But I noticed that [Jane] was gone. I looked out my window, and my car was gone. I went outside and finally saw her driving up, still in her robe. I said, 'Where have you been?' She said, 'I . . . I . . . it just occurred to me that they [could have] put a bomb in that car last night, and if you had gotten in there you would have been blown away. So I got up and drove it. It's all right.'"

A man is fortunate indeed when his wife is his devoted helper—whether she bakes him a cake, soothes his aching muscles, or even puts her life on the line for him. No role demonstrates more beautifully the way Jesus shows His love for each of us. — James C. Dobson and Shirley Dobson, *Night Light: A Devotional for Couples* (Carol Stream, IL: Tyndale, 2011).

17. What do we learn about sex from the creation story?

In previous generations, some people believed women were not supposed to enjoy sex. Even today some Christians still feel that sex between marital partners is somehow sinful or "dirty." But there's nothing biblical about either viewpoint.

The Lord created us as sexual beings and gave us the gift of physical intimacy as a means for expressing love between husband and wife. In the biblical account of the Garden of Eden, we are told that "a man will leave his father and mother and be united to his wife, and they will become one flesh." The Bible says that before sin entered the picture, the first husband and wife were unashamed of their nakedness (Genesis 2:24–25).

Scripture also uses sexual symbolism to describe the relationship between God and man. (Look, for example, at Isaiah 62:5; Jeremiah 7:9 and 23:10; Ezekiel 16; Hosea; Ephesians 5; and Revelation 19:6–7.) In addition, Solomon's Song of Songs clearly celebrates sexual pleasure between married lovers. We suggest that you set time aside to read that book together.

As designed by God, sexual desire in marriage is more than an afterthought or a means to guarantee procreation. That's why we can wholeheartedly say, "Let's 'make love' the way our God intended!" — James C. Dobson and Shirley Dobson, *Night Light: A Devotional for Couples* (Carol Stream, IL: Tyndale, 2011).

18. Besides having kids, what is God's purpose for sex?

Sex joins two people spiritually and emotionally as well as physically. This is its purpose — to bond a couple together. Sex connects and fuses people together. It's sticky. Similarly, if you're stuck to someone and you try to pull loose, it's going to hurt. You're both going to leave pieces of yourselves behind. (Remind me to tell you a tragic story about my kids' pet hamster, Fuzzy, and his life-changing accident with one of those super-glue-strip kind of mousetraps. Ouch. Or the time my younger sister came screaming, "There's a dog stuck to our dog—and I can't get them apart!") — Craig Groeschel, *Weird: Because Normal Isn't Working* (Grand Rapids, MI: Zondervan, 2011).

19. What do you want to recall from today's discussion?

20. How can we support one another in prayer this week?

Genesis, Lesson #3
Good Questions Have Small Groups Talking
www.joshhunt.com

Genesis 3.1 - 19

OPEN

Let's each your name and one thing you are grateful for.

DIG

1. What do we learn about our enemy, the devil, from this passage?

Satan introduced doubt. That is his number one tactic. He comes to each of us, saying, "Has God indeed said … ?" If he can snare us with doubt, he has us quickly and immediately. And so many people capitulate at this very point. They cave in to doubt. They don't know enough about the Word of God to stand strong and say, "Listen, Satan, this is what God has indeed said!"

Eve, however, was not ignorant of God's word. She did not give in to Satan at the introduction of doubt. Eve responded with a clear statement of God's instructions. What I want you to notice is that Eve knew and understood precisely what she was not to do. She did not act out of ignorance or confusion. She was not mixed up. She knew the rule and its consequence.

Note what Satan said next. Then the serpent said to the woman, "You will not surely die. For God knows that in the day you eat of it your eyes will be opened, and you will be like God, knowing good and evil" (Gen. 3:4–5). — Charles F.

Stanley, *Our Unmet Needs* (Nashville, TN: T. Nelson, 1999), 139.

2. As Christians, should we study the devil?

C. S. Lewis once said that there are two errors we can make concerning the devil. One is to disbelieve he exists; the other is to take an unhealthy overinterest in the demonic realm. Where do we see these two tendencies in our cultures? Use this study to keep matters in perspective. — R.C. Sproul, *Before the Face of God: Book 2: A Daily Guide for Living from the Gospel of Luke*, electronic ed. (Grand Rapids: Baker Book House; Ligonier Ministries, 1993).

3. 2 Corinthians 2.11. What did Paul teach about the study of the devil?

Here, we see Paul's exhortation to be knowledgeable concerning Satan's devices—one of which is not only to get someone to sin, but to make him feel terrible about his sin, and to cause division among believers concerning the issue of his sin. Paul says to the church at Corinth, "Don't let Satan ostracize this one who needs to come back into your midst. And don't let him divide you in the process." — Jon Courson, *Jon Courson's Application Commentary* (Nashville, TN: Thomas Nelson, 2003), 1107.

4. Where did Satan come from?

God originally created Lucifer with the power of "free will" so that he could voluntarily worship and exalt God. But Lucifer used his power of choice to exalt himself. First it was pride ("lest being puffed up with pride he fall into the same condemnation as the devil" [1 Tim. 3:6]). Second, in unbelief, he rebelled against God. Lucifer did not believe that God could know what he was doing or judge him. Third, in self-deception, Lucifer actually believed he could wrestle the throne away from the Almighty. Finally, there was an unwillingness on the part of Lucifer to abide in the stead where he had been placed by the Creator. After the fall Lucifer is also called "great dragon . . . that serpent of old . . . the Devil and Satan" (Rev. 12:9). — Elmer Towns, *Bible*

Answers for Almost All Your Questions (Nashville: Thomas Nelson, 2003).

5. What does Satan do? How does he do it?

There's a story about a farmer who was frustrated by thieves who were constantly stealing his watermelons. He finally came up with a brilliant plan to thwart the thieves. He poisoned one watermelon and then put a sign in his watermelon field that read, "Warning—one of these watermelons has been poisoned."

The next day the farmer went out and discovered that none of his melons had been stolen because the thieves didn't know which one was poisoned. He was satisfied that his idea had worked and that the problem was solved.

But two days later the farmer came out to his field to find that his sign had been altered. Someone had changed it to read, "Two of these watermelons have been poisoned." The farmer had to destroy his entire crop because he didn't know which other melon was poisoned.

That's often what it is like in dealing with the devil. When you come up with a plan, he seems to come up with something better. When you put up a sign, he changes the wording. Regardless of the strategy you devise, you just can't outwit the devil. E.M. Bounds offers a helpful perspective.

> The Devil is a very busy character. He does a big business, a very ugly business, but he does it well, that is, as well as an ugly business can be done. He has lots of experience, big brains, a black heart, great force, tireless energy, and is of great influence and great character. All his immense resources are used for evil purposes.

Whether we know it or not, "We are opposed by a living, intelligent, resourceful and cunning enemy who can outlive the oldest Christian, outwork the busiest, outfight the strongest and outwit the wisest."

Ephesians 6:11 refers to "the schemes of the devil." The Greek word translated "schemes" is methodeias. The word is plural, so we know that Satan employs many methods and schemes to undermine our lives and ministries.

> The devil's brain is prolific with plans. He has many ways of doing many things. Perhaps he has many ways of doing each thing. With him nothing is stereotyped. He never runs in ruts. Fruitful, diverse, and ever fresh is his way of doing things. Indirect, cunning, and graceful are his plans. He acts by trickery, and always by guile.

Second Corinthians 2:10-11 also refers to Satan's schemes, but here the Greek word is noema, which means "thought" or "purpose." Satan is feverishly implementing his methods, plans, and purposes. The Bible is clear that Satan is engaged in a multitude of nefarious activities. He destroys, deceives, discourages, demoralizes, disheartens, and distorts. He counterfeits, masquerades, clouds with illusion, and sows seeds of doubt.

Satan's main method is to disguise sin to make it appealing and attractive. He makes sin look good and seduces us to believe we have the ability to control our sin and its consequences. Satan tries to sabotage our contentment in Christ and convince us that he can offer something better. He lures the unsuspecting with the promise of happiness, but he hides the price that must be paid. Erwin Lutzer poignantly describes this ploy. — Mark Hitchcock, *101 Answers to Questions about Satan, Demons, and Spiritual Warfare* (Eugene, OR: Harvest House, 2014).

6. What will eventually happen to Satan?

Satan made his entrance on the stage of human history in Genesis 3 when he tempted Adam and Eve in the Garden of Eden. He will make his inglorious exit in Revelation 20:10 when he is finally cast into the lake of fire, where the Antichrist and the false prophet are confined. As the great reformer Martin Luther reminds us,

The Prince of Darkness grim,
We tremble not for him;
His rage we can endure,
For lo, his doom is sure;
One little word shall fell him.

Mark Hitchcock, *101 Answers to Questions about Satan, Demons, and Spiritual Warfare* (Eugene, OR: Harvest House, 2014).

7. Back to Genesis 3. Notice the word "really" in verse 1. What do we learn from this about Satan and how he tempts us?

If you're a Christian, you know that getting sidetracked from God is easy. Most do. It's perfectly normal. And you'll find lots of outside help for your heart to wander, lots of things to distract you. As you notice how people around you are living, you might find yourself questioning whether it's even worth it to follow God. It may seem like not many other people are following him. And according to Matthew 7:13 – 14, many people aren't. Perhaps worse, it seems like the people who do follow God are, well ... honestly, weird. According to that passage in Matthew 7, they're the few who are willing to do it.

Where do these kinds of thoughts come from? Have you ever considered that they might come from your spiritual enemy? Although we looked at this earlier, it's worth mentioning again: Jesus clearly identifies Satan's explicit mission — to steal, kill, and destroy (John 10:10). If you allow your enemy to steal your faith, he can destroy your life and ultimately kill your relationship with God. He's the great deceiver, the father of lies (John 8:44), so we need to be wise to his tricks (2 Cor. 2:11).

Satan specializes in destroying people's faith. And he's been using the same technique to do it — an extremely effective approach — from the very beginning. When he came to Eve in the form of a serpent, he planted the smallest seed of doubt in the ready soil of her mind. He said, "Did God really say ..." (Gen. 3:1, emphasis mine). Then he lied to her, essentially saying that it was God who was the liar and that God was keeping something from her (vv. 4 – 5). In other words, he weakened Eve's faith by questioning God's authority. And then he simply waited. And watched his seed grow and blossom and bear its deadly fruit.

Paul referred to this same attack when he wrote with heartfelt concern to the church at Corinth: "I am afraid that just as Eve was deceived by the serpent's cunning, your minds may somehow be led astray from your sincere and pure devotion to Christ" (2 Cor. 11:3). I feel that same concern. If you've been close to God in the past but feel distant from him now, isn't that exactly how it played out? Maybe you didn't even realize it was happening, but somehow you woke up one day and found you'd drifted. You'd been led astray from your faith in Christ. — Craig Groeschel, *Weird: Because Normal Isn't Working* (Grand Rapids, MI: Zondervan, 2011).

8. What is the lesson for us? What do we learn about dealing with the devil from this passage?

"Are you sure you heard God right?" Satan asked Eve. The Fall of mankind began with a question. The same is still true. Even in Christian circles, Satan's strategy is to get believers to doubt their ability to understand the Word. Don't fall prey to his tactics, gang. The Word of God is incredibly profound. But it is also amazingly simple. — Jon Courson, *Jon Courson's Application Commentary: Volume One: Genesis–Job* (Nashville, TN: Thomas Nelson, 2005),

9. How was Satan trying to make Eve feel about God? What is the lesson for us?

I find it interesting that the devil didn't deny that God had spoken to Eve. Rather than challenging the fact that God had spoken, he twisted God's words to say something the Creator had never intended. In so doing, of course, he was questioning God's fairness and love for Eve: Why would God make trees with fruit, and then forbid you to eat the fruit? Does that make sense? If God really loved you, He would let you eat of this tree, too. Why is He holding out on you?

It's not fair. God must not love you to keep something this important from you.

Maybe you've felt that way before—or possibly feel that way now. Maybe you feel as though God is holding something back from you that you think you really need right now. Just remember, if God says "no", then He does so for your own good.

We wrestle with that thought, don't we? It's a little difficult for us to process sometimes. But consider the way you would deal with young children. You wouldn't let them live entirely on sugar, watch cartoons all day, stay up all night, or play tag on the freeway, even though they think they need to do these things. Instead, you set certain limits, because you know what's good for them (and much better than they know themselves).

God does the same with us. In His wisdom and far-seeing love, He says "no" to certain things. But if God says "no", then it is the right thing—and the best thing for us. Psalm 84:11 says, "No good thing will He withhold from those who walk uprightly." In other words, God isn't in the business of withholding good and helpful things from His children. If He does tell me to avoid something, then it's because He knows it would harm me. If He says, "Don't do this. It's not good," then we must take His word for it. — Greg Laurie, *Daily Hope for Hurting Hearts: A Devotional* (Dana Point, CA: Kerygma Publishing—Allen David Books, 2011).

10. Why didn't God let them eat of this tree? What do we learn about God from this? What is the lesson for us?

What do you think God's love is? Do you envision a permissive love that allows you to do whatever you want? That doesn't describe the love of God. You see, God loves you enough to put restrictions in your life. He loves you enough to say, "Do this. It will help you. And don't do this. It's bad for you."

Suppose a child asks his mother, "Mommy, can I play in the street?" Of course she would say, "No, you may not. I love you and don't want you to be in a place where you would be endangered. One day, you will realize that I did this not from a lack of love, but because I do love you."

It's the same with us. When God says "no" to us, it's not because He doesn't love us. It's just the opposite.

In the Garden of Eden, God told Adam, "'Of every tree of the garden you may freely eat; but of the tree of the knowledge of good and evil you shall not eat, for in the day that you eat of it you shall surely die'" (Genesis 2:16-17). So the devil tempted Eve: "Has God indeed said, 'You shall not eat of every tree of the garden?'" (Genesis 3:1). Essentially he was saying, "If God really loved you, then He would let you do whatever you want." The truth was that because God loved Adam and Eve, He didn't want them to fall into sin. Yet they disobeyed God and that's exactly what happened.

Those limits that you find in the pages of the Bible are there for your own good. God has put a fence around you, so to speak. But it's not to keep you confined—it's to keep you safe from the many dangers in this world—and in the invisible spiritual world that surrounds us. — Greg Laurie, *Daily Hope for Hurting Hearts: A Devotional* (Dana Point, CA: Kerygma Publishing—Allen David Books, 2011).

11. Verse 2, 3. How did Eve change what God said? Why is this important? What is the lesson for us?

In answering the serpent, Eve made three changes in what God said, slight changes to be sure, but changes that opened the door to sin. First, God had said, "You may freely eat" but the woman simply said, "We may eat," minimizing the privileges (cf. 2:16–17; 3:2–3). Secondly, with her focus on the prohibition she added to it "or even touch it." Third, and most seriously, she lessened the emphasis on punishment by saying "lest you die" (rather than the stronger expression, "You shall surely die," which God had used). That this failure to preserve the exact words of God was at the heart of the temptation is clear from the response of the serpent, for when he heard what she said, he replied, "You won't die!" (The construction is unusual, with the negative particle placed blatantly in front of the very words God used of the penalty in 2:17.) Since she was not convinced of the certainty of death for sin, he was free to deny it (3:4). This is why Jesus explained that Satan was a liar from the beginning (John 8:44). The lie is that people can sin and get away with it. But death is the penalty of sin (2:17), as the man and the woman would immediately discover. — Allen Ross and John N. Oswalt, *Cornerstone Biblical Commentary: Genesis, Exodus, vol. 1* (Carol Stream, IL: Tyndale House Publishers, 2008), 51–52.

12. Notice the phrase, "and you must not touch it." What do we learn about Satan and how he tempts us from this?

Eve's subtle shift in heart was further revealed in her telltale addition to God's word: "But God [Elohim] said, 'You shall not eat of the fruit of the tree that is in the midst of the garden, neither shall you touch it' " (v. 3a, italics added). God never said, "neither shall you touch it"! Eve magnified God's strictness—"Just touch the tree, and zap!—you're dead!" Her comment suggested that God is so harsh that an inadvertent slip would bring death.

This is so typical of us sons and daughters of Eve. A father says to his young daughter, "You and your friend Katie have been too noisy—so Katie will have to go home." Then his daughter runs to her mother crying, "Daddy says I can't ever have Katie over again!" The boss calls in an employee who's been late several times and says, "I think this is something you need to give attention to. It's important." The employee walks out of the office and says to his coworkers, "You know what that stuffed shirt said? If I'm late again, I'm fired!" When we don't like a prohibition or a warning, we magnify its strictness. The suggestion that our superior is unjust mitigates our culpability. And if we do not perform, we may imagine that we have a morally superior way out.

We must beware, lest we begin to think that God's word is unreasonable or too requiring. Do we find ourselves overstating Scripture's call to purity as "unrealistic"? Have we represented the Bible's teaching on forgiveness as impracticable? If so, we need to take a step back and a deep breath—and pray. — R. Kent Hughes, *Genesis: Beginning and Blessing, Preaching the Word* (Wheaton, IL: Crossway Books, 2004), 68.

13. Satan statement was, in a way, an accusation against God. What was Satan accusing God of?

But the tempter went a step further and raised doubts about God's character. He implied that God was wrongly jealous, holding the humans back from their full potential which was to be like God, "knowing both good and evil" (3:5). So Satan held out for them the promise of divinity with the power to alter life. — Allen Ross and John N. Oswalt, *Cornerstone Biblical Commentary: Genesis, Exodus, vol. 1* (Carol Stream, IL: Tyndale House Publishers, 2008), 52.

14. Verse 5. What is the temptation to want to be like God? What is that about? Again, what is the lesson for us?

Much like Elijah, we can be tempted to think we are the only one really faithful, the only special or gifted or entitled one. This is related to that old temptation "you will be like God," for when we think of ourselves as god-like, we become obsessed with our own success and happiness and need to prop up an inflated sense of our competence and worth. Then reality hits, and often when this idealized me crumbles, what is left is a deflated, "shattered" me. Like Adam and Eve, we want to run and hide. We think that we have nothing to offer and that everything is awful.

But the Spirit wants to liberate us, both from thinking as if we are God and from thinking as if we are nothing. There is a God; it is not you. He wants to help you be the real you, the best version of you. He wants to help you become you-ier. — John Ortberg, *The Me I Want to Be* (Grand Rapids, MI: Zondervan, 2010).

15. Verse 7. What changed after the fall?

After eating the fruit, the first human pair lose their innocence and two new emotions grip them; fear and shame. They attempt to deal with their shame by using fig leaves, and their fear drives them to hide among the trees of the garden. These strategies fail; fig leaves do not remove shame and it is not possible to hide from God. Since all else has failed, they resort to passing the blame. — James McKeown, *Genesis, The Two Horizons Old Testament Commentary* (Grand Rapids, MI; Cambridge, U.K.: William B. Eerdmans Publishing Company, 2008), 35.

16. Verses 8, 9. What do we learn about God from these verses?

One of the most amazing, gracious, humble things about God is that he wants so much to be in a freely chosen, love relationship with human beings that he will allow us to hide from him if we want to. But think about that for a moment. This is God, who is omniscient—there is nothing he does not know. He is omnipresent—there's not one square inch of the universe that he does not occupy. Is trying to hide from God a real smart strategy?

God says, "Hey, son, hey, daughter, where are you? Won't you just come to me? Won't you just tell me everything?" You need to know that God promises to accept you fully, to forgive you utterly.

Our part is to stop hiding. Just come out and say, "All right, God, I'm going to tell you everything. I'm going to pour my heart out to you—all the good and all the bad—and I'll receive your forgiveness and your acceptance as a gift of grace."

To anyone who does this, to anyone who receives the gift of forgiveness, God says, "Come home. I know all about you. I love you. I'll walk with you through this life, and be with you for all of eternity. You're fully known. You're fully loved." — John Ortberg, *Now What? God's Guide to Life for Graduates* (Grand Rapids, MI: Zondervan, 2011).

17. Verse 10. Why is Adam afraid? Should he be afraid?

What does God do in response to the rebellion of Adam and Eve? God enters the Garden and shouts, "Adam! Eve! Where are you? It's time for our daily walk" (see Gen. 3:9).

What? How is that even possible? They've just spit in the face of God by doing the one and only thing they were commanded not to do. If ever there was a time for God to break out the stick, this is it, right? But that's not what happens. God lovingly, intimately, warmly moves toward them. They are sinful, broken, confused, and running. They have rejected God, yet God does not reject them. There will be a number of aftereffects from Adam and Eve's disobedience, but God rejecting them is not one of them.

Here we get absolute clarity about the true nature of God. We see the lie, and we see the truth.

The lie is that God has rejected us. The lie is that God is distant from us. The lie is that God is punishing us for our sin.
— Daniel Hill, John Ortberg, and Nancy Ortberg, *10:10: Life to the Fullest* (Grand Rapids, MI: Baker, 2014).

18. Verses 12, 13. What do we learn about ourselves from these verses? What is the application?

If you struggle with blame, you are not alone. To some extent, it is part of the human condition, and you come by it honestly. Our parents, Adam and Eve, modeled and passed the trait down through the generations: "The woman you put here with me—she gave me some fruit from the tree, and I ate it. . . . The serpent deceived me, and I ate" (Genesis 3:12–13). They pointed the finger of blame on the Devil, each other, and even God. Even then, blame did not work for them. They stayed on the hot seat. God did not relinquish his righteous stance, but followed through with severe consequences for their disobedience.

Watch children grow in their blaming skills; it is so natural. When they are in trouble, they constantly scan the horizon, seeking someone to blame for their difficulties. "I am in time-out because Mom is mean; the dog ate my homework; Billy made me push him." Given our heritage and makeup, it is no small wonder that we are a species of blamers.

What is blaming? It is ascribing responsibility to someone for a fault. When we accuse another of a problem, we are blaming. Blame is not bad in and of itself. It has a good function. Blame separates out who is truly responsible for what in a problem, so that we are able to know how to solve it. It helps differentiate between what is our fault, and what is another's. For example, your girlfriend may have invited you to a party at which her ex is also attending. She was vague about whether or not he would be there. But you also gave the impression that it wouldn't bother you, which wasn't true. So you have a miserable time at the party. As you blame, you figure out that she was at fault for not being clear. You were at fault for not being honest about your feelings. You both know what your growth tasks are to resolve this kind of issue. Blame helped point the way to the solutions. — Henry Cloud and John Townsend, *Boundaries in Dating: How Healthy Choices Grow Healthy Relationships* (Grand Rapids, MI: Zondervan, 2009).

19. What harm comes our way when we play the blame game?

You can get so caught up in the blame game that you lose all momentum in the pursuit of your goals. You can blame others and refuse to forgive others who hurt you all you like, but the truth remains:

- You are responsible for your actions, responses, and feelings.

- There is never any justification in hurting someone else, harboring unforgiveness, or taking vengeance into your own hands.

- You have a choice rooted in your free will about what you choose to do in the face of persecution, injury, criticism, or hurt feelings.

- The blame game always hurts you more than it hurts others. The blame game stunts your spiritual growth, damages your fellowship with God, and promotes disharmony with others.

When you continually blame others, you actually choose to live in a state of unforgiveness. You hold others responsible for your pain, and you refuse to forgive them for what they have done to you. As long as you refuse to forgive, you cannot be forgiven (Luke 6:37). Jesus was very clear on this point. You must forgive others if you are to receive God's forgiveness.

Many years ago, a man I know loaned a friend twelve thousand dollars, which was a significant amount to him at that time and represented virtually all of his savings. His friend mismanaged the money and lost it all. Not only that, but he began to bad-mouth the friend who had loaned him the money and disassociated himself completely from their friendship. The man faced a question, How should he respond to the borrower?

He talked it over with another friend one day, and the friend said, "Well, you know you're going to have to forgive him." The man said, "Forgive him? After what he did?" But the seed of God's truth had been planted. The more the man prayed about that situation and read God's Word, the more he knew he had to forgive the man and go on.

He forgave that man in a specific prayer and intentional prayer of forgiveness. It was a day of tremendous freedom and victory for him. And what did the Lord do? Within a year, the Lord had restored every penny that man had loaned. Not only did he experience financial restoration, but he had joy and peace in his heart that he had done the right thing before God.

He was able to move forward, without any hindrance in his faith or in his pursuit of his goals. What could have been a major disappointment or stumbling block to him had been removed.

As long as you live in a state of unforgiveness toward those who wrong you, the Lord cannot bless you and cause your efforts to prosper. I'm not referring to being born again here: I'm referring to refusing to forgive the sins of those who hurt, injure, reject, or criticize you. Choose to forgive! You will release yourself to move forward toward God's goals for your life. — Charles F. Stanley, *Success God's Way* (Nashville: T. Nelson Publishers, 2000).

20. What good comes to those who don't blame—those who take 100% responsibility for their lives?

The fight to take responsibility occurs within. And rarely does talent, intelligence, or opportunity make the difference in whether a person wins that battle. It calls for character. That's why Stewart B. Johnson remarked, "Our business in life is not to get ahead of others, but to get ahead of ourselves— to break our own records, to outstrip our yesterday by our today."

You can tell when people develop deeper character, accept responsibility for themselves, and begin learning from their failures. It really shows in their performance. For example, I observed that in Chris Chandler of the NFL's Atlanta Falcons after I moved to Georgia.

Chandler is a quarterback who had a history of floating from team to team. Prior to his employment with Atlanta, he had played for five teams in nine years, and he had never excelled. But everything started to change for him in Phoenix. That's where he met Jerry Rhome.

"I was at a point where I really didn't care anymore," says Chandler about that part of his career. His view of the league affected his willingness to take full responsibility for his lack of success. "I thought the NFL was just totally political, and I was ready to quit. Jerry brought back my competitiveness, and he taught me how to play. He made it fun again."

How did Rhome accomplish that? He told Chandler the truth. "I told him after the season that he had a lot of ability, but he was uncoachable," said Rhome, "and I offered to work with him."

At first Chandler resisted. He expected everyone else to adjust to his style and ability. But then he changed his mind and accepted Rhome's offer. With help, hard work, and a new willingness to change himself rather than expecting others to change, Chandler has become one of the best quarterbacks in the NFL, taking his team to the Super Bowl in 1999. — John C. Maxwell, *Failing Forward* (Thomas Nelson Publishers, 2000).

21. What do you want to recall from today's discussion?

22. How can we support one another in prayer this week?

Genesis, Lesson #4
Good Questions Have Small Groups Talking
www.joshhunt.com

Genesis 6:8-18; 7:11-14

OPEN

Let's each your name and when is the last time you were on a boat?

DIG

1. **What was the world like back in the day—in the days of Noah?**

    We find in Genesis 6 that the earth was full of corruption and violence. It says that "everything they thought or imagined was consistently and totally evil" (Gen. 6:5 NLT) and that "everyone on earth was corrupt" (Gen. 6:12 NLT). Everyone on the earth was corrupt. — Craig Groeschel, *What Is God Really like? Expanded Edition* (Grand Rapids, MI: Zondervan, 2010).

2. **What was Noah like?**

    The character of Noah is then defined. First, he is called a 'righteous' man. That word, ṣadîq, means 'to conform to a moral or ethical standard'. In other words, Noah was one who recognized and observed his responsibilities to God and to his fellow man. It does not mean that he was sinless, for 'All have sinned and fall short of the glory of God' (Rom. 3:23). It does mean, on the other hand, that he lived an exemplary life.

Noah is also characterized as 'blameless in his time'. He was an exception to his age, which was filled with such wickedness (see Ezek. 14:14, 20). To be blameless does not mean that a person is sinless. It really signifies one who has integrity and honour, one with an upright heart that attempts to follow the ways of Yahweh.

Finally, the text says that 'Noah walked with God'. This expression was used of Enoch in 5:22, 24. Like Enoch, Noah had a close fellowship and communion with God. In the Hebrew sentence structure 'with God' opens the sentence. This inversion is an aspect of 'the Hebrew word order [which] gives God pride of place in the sentence, thus accentuating the fact that the standards by which Noah's righteousness is judged are divine, not human'. — John D. Currid, *A Study Commentary on Genesis: Genesis 1:1–25:18, vol. 1, EP Study Commentary* (Darlington, England: Evangelical Press, n.d.), 182–183.

3. Genesis 6.8. What does it mean that Noah found favor in the eyes of the Lord?

"Noah found grace in the eyes of the Lord" (Gen. 6:8 KJV). If you look in some of the other translations, it says, "Noah found favor with the Lord." You know what that word favor or grace is? It means "to be charmed by." When God looked at Noah's life, he saw something that he liked. It's similar to when I looked at my wife, Saralynn, when we were dating. I saw something I liked—she "charmed" me.

That's a gift. When we're standing on our own, frankly, there's not much that God can see that he would like about us, is there? If it were not for his gift of grace, God would have no reason to see anything in me that he liked, because on my own I'm rebellious. On my own I have my plan. On my own I have my agenda. On my own I want to do things my way, not God's way. And on my own I'm not afraid to shake my fist in God's face and say, "I'm on my own." If not for the gift of grace I'd have nothing to offer, nothing to give back to God.

In Ephesians, Paul wrote a couple of lines about this that have become very familiar among Christians. Maybe you could even quote them: "For it is by grace you have been saved, through faith — and this not from yourselves, it is the gift of God — not by works, so that no one can boast" (Eph. 2:8 — 9).

I don't have anything worth boasting about outside of God. Sure, I could probably get a good job and make a bunch of money and have a nice house and a big family and a manicured lawn, and I could probably have a lot of "stuff." But if I were to stand before God with a bunch of physical stuff, what would I really have to boast about? Outside of God and his gift of grace, there's nothing. In Galatians 2:21 Paul goes to the extent that he says, "I do not set aside the grace of God, for if righteousness could be gained through the law, Christ died for nothing!" — Craig Groeschel, *What Is God Really like? Expanded Edition* (Grand Rapids, MI: Zondervan, 2010).

4. What about everyone else? Did they find grace in the eyes of the Lord?

That Noah found grace in the eyes of the Lord does not mean that God showed grace to Noah exclusively. Yes, a flood wiped everyone else out eventually, but not before God gave them one hundred years to repent of their wickedness and receive salvation. Yes, the planet was deluged, but every man had opportunity to hear His message as they observed Noah building the huge barge. But the world refused to grab hold of the good news of salvation, and they drowned in their sin. It wasn't that God looked at Noah with grace and everyone else with condemnation. God looked at everyone with eyes of grace and mercy. It's just that Noah found the grace.

The question I want to ask you today is this: What have you found in the eyes of the Lord?

> A London traffic jam prevented C. S. Lewis from arriving at a certain religious symposium on time. The panel, comprised of the world's most highly esteemed religious thinkers, began without him, their first question being:

What is unique about Christianity? Although the Buddhist, Muslim, Jew, and Taoist discussed the question they could arrive at no conclusive answer. In the midst of their debate, C. S. Lewis burst into the room.

"Dr. Lewis," said the moderator, "tell us what is unique to Christianity."

"That's easy," Lewis replied. "It's grace."

C. S. Lewis was right. No other religion or philosophy provides unmerited, undeserved, unearned favor. Every other religion, every other philosophy says there are things we must do—devotional exercises, good deeds, or righteous acts—to earn blessings from Allah or to gain favor from Buddha. Only biblical Christianity says, "It's all grace, nothing more, nothing less, nothing else." — Jon Courson, *Jon Courson's Application Commentary: Volume One: Genesis–Job* (Nashville, TN: Thomas Nelson, 2005), 31.

5. How can we find favor in the eyes of the Lord?

I have this conversation with people all the time. "Is there a place, maybe after I die, that I have to go so that I can finish paying off some of my sin before I can get into heaven?" Some churches teach that if you're not completely sinless when you die, there is a period of time that you have to go though to purge yourself of sin before you can enter God's presence in heaven. And whenever somebody talks to me about that and asks if that is really true, I say, "Let me ask you this question: if I still have to pay for my sin before I can get to heaven after I die, why did Christ die? Why did he die if I'm still responsible for all my sin? What exactly did he do on that cross if I still have to pay for my own sin?" God's grace is not about what I do or what I don't do; it's about what he did. If we can rely on the first level, if we can fix it ourselves with first-level support—just what we come up with, just what the philosophers say, just what the songwriters come up with — then why in the world did he die?

When Paul wrote to the Galatians they thought they could ask God to forgive them and everything would be cool, but they still had to follow all of the Old Testament laws. So, he actually asked them in Chapter 3, "Let me get this straight. You started your spiritual life with the God and the Spirit of God and Jesus Christ, but now you have to finish it yourselves? Is that what you're telling me? God is big enough and Jesus' death is big enough to start your salvation but is not big enough to finish it? You have to finish it on your own?" He said, "Don't set aside God's grace; it's a gift." We don't earn it, we don't deserve it, there's nothing we can do for it. God said, "Here. You humans are my prize creation, and I'm going to offer you second-level support that is far beyond what you could do on your own — the man, Christ Jesus. I'm going to make it available to you completely, and I'm going to make it available to you freely as a gift." — Craig Groeschel, *What Is God Really like? Expanded Edition* (Grand Rapids, MI: Zondervan, 2010).

6. Try to imagine what Noah felt like—like the only righteous one on the planet. Do you ever feel that way?

Learn, too, that solitary goodness is possible. Noah stood uninfected by the universal contagion; and, as is always the case, the evil around, which he did not share, drove him to a more rigid abstinence from it. A Christian who is alone 'in his generations,' like a lily among nettles, has to be, and usually is, a more earnest Christian than if he were among like-minded men. The saints in 'Caesar's household' needed to be very unmistakable saints, if they were not to be swept away by the torrent of godlessness. It is hard, but it is possible, for a boy at school, or a young man in an office, or a soldier in a barrack, to stand alone, and be Christlike; but only on condition that he yields to no temptation to drop his conduct to the level around him, and is never guilty of compromise. Once yield, and all is over. Flowers grow on a dunghill, and the very reeking rottenness may make the bloom finer. — Alexander MacLaren, *Expositions of Holy Scripture: Genesis* (Bellingham, WA: Logos Bible Software, 2009), 49–50.

7. Verse 15. How big was Noah's ark?

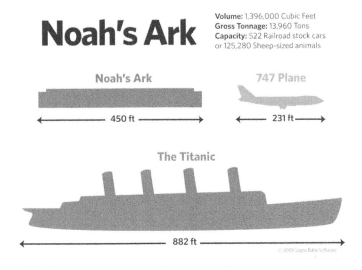

8. It is always a good idea to read the Bible with emotion—that is, read the Bible asking what the people were feeling. What do you think Noah felt like as God spoke to him about this ark?

The ark was of incredible size, especially in its ancient setting. When Noah laid out its keel at 450 feet, the pre-diluvians must have laughed themselves silly. We can visualize it by imagining the length of one and a half football fields! It was 238 feet longer than the Cutty Sark, the largest wooden boat ever built, at 212 feet. Of course, in modern times the advent of steel has made possible much larger vessels. The Queen Elizabeth was over 1,000 feet in length.

What a monster the ark was! As best we can tell, the ark was shaped like a shallow box topped with a roof, with an eighteen-inch space under the roof interrupted only by the roof supports, so light could get into the vessel from every side. Noah had more than enough work to keep him and his three sons occupied for a century. Remember, there were no trucks, no chain saws, and no cranes. — R. Kent

Hughes, *Genesis: Beginning and Blessing, Preaching the Word* (Wheaton, IL: Crossway Books, 2004), 135.

9. Try to imagine how Noah's neighbors treated Noah when he started building this ark. What do we learn about following God from this?

Building the ark required careful planning and engineering and a century of sweat, but "Noah did this; he did all that God commanded him" (v. 22). When Noah finished laying out the incredible 450-foot keel and began to install the ark's ribs, imagine the abuse he took! How many Noah jokes do you think people could come up with in a century? Imagine the taunts that came at the expense of Noah and his own: "How many of Noah's sons does it take to drive a spike? One to hold the spike, and one to ..." But Noah remained obedient, doing exactly what God said, for twenty-five ... fifty ... seventy-five ... a hundred years—until the ark lay like a huge coffin on the land.

And beyond the ridicule there was the settled hatred of a demonized culture and its fallen ones, the violent "men of renown." When they saw that the ark was meant to save Noah and his family, some undoubtedly flew into a homicidal rage. Noah's preaching of righteousness would have brought death apart from God's protective hand. Finally at the end, as Noah brought supplies into the high and dry ark and collected the animals, we read twice that it all happened "as God had commanded Noah" (7:9, 16). The words everything and all describe Noah's obedience.

So now we begin to see what it means to be righteous. The righteous person rests everything on the bare word of God and obeys it. We also glimpse what it means to walk with God, because to walk with him is not a stroll. It means to go the same way in obedience—even as the culture marches the other way. What is the person God saves like? He believes in God's promise to him, and it is counted as righteousness. As a righteous man he lives not a perfect but a blameless life. He walks with God. And everything about him is covered by obedience to God's perfect word. — R. Kent Hughes, *Genesis:*

Beginning and Blessing, Preaching the Word (Wheaton, IL: Crossway Books, 2004), 137.

10. Genesis 6.18. What is a covenant?

Once we are in a relationship with God, paramount knowledge of the bare essentials of that relationship is required, in order to be able to both understand and nurture it. Here, I am talking about the covenant relationship with God, where God promises divine blessings if we walk with Him in His word. The history of this biblical form of relationship stems from God's covenant with Noah and Abraham.

What then is a covenant? A covenant is a promise. God made promises with His people so that, although God was going to destroy the world by flood, due to Noah's righteousness, God spared Noah and his family's lives; by instructing Noah to build an ark of cypress wood and to take inside the ark certain animals and told him, "I will establish my covenant with you" (Gen 6:18). And with Abraham, God instructed him to get out of his country, and his father's house, to a land that He would show him and said "I will make you a great nation; I will bless you and make your name great" (Gen. 12:1-2). He promised to give Abraham the land of Canaan in Genesis 15. These covenants are discussed fully in chapter three below. Suffice it to say, the covenants, as we see, were made between a superior party, God, and inferior party, Noah/Abraham (man) both of whom were not in any position to bargain or haggle over the terms of the promises.

Note that the Lord did not set any conditions for man to observe except to obey His instructions. How reassuring it is to know God's covenant is established with us. He is faithful to keep to His word and would thus keep us safe through our relationship with Him. What are His instructions, one may ask? And how are they applicable to us today? — Olawunmi Biriyok, *Walk the Walk* (Maitland, FL: Xulon Press, 2013).

11. Genesis 7.2. Why do you think Noah was to take more clean animals than unclean?

This was the basis of a lawsuit years ago against Dr. Harry Rimmer who had offered a thousand dollars to anyone who could show a contradiction in the Bible. There were several liberal theologians who testified in a court of law that this was a contradiction. Why would it first say two of each kind and now seven of each kind? Of course Dr. Rimmer won the lawsuit. All you have to do is turn over to see that when Noah got out of the ark, he offered clean beasts as sacrifices. Where would he have gotten the clean beasts if he had not taken more than two? It was only of the clean beasts that he took seven, and now we know why. Those that were not clean went in by twos, a male and a female. — *Thru The Bible with J. Vernon McGee.*

12. How could Noah's ark hold hundreds of thousands of species?

PROBLEM: The Bible says Noah's ark was only 45 feet high, 75 feet wide, and 450 feet long (Gen. 6:15, NIV). Noah was told to take two of every kind of unclean animal and seven of every kind of clean animal (6:19; 7:2). But scientists inform us that there are between one half a billion to over a billion species of animals.

SOLUTION: First, the modern concept of "species" is not the same as a "kind" in the Bible. There are probably only several hundred different "kinds" of land animals that would have to be taken into the ark. The sea animals stayed in the sea, and many species could have survived in egg form. Second, the ark was not small; it was a huge structure—the size of a modern ocean liner. Furthermore, it had three stories (6:16) which tripled its space to a total of over 1.5 million cubic feet!

Third, Noah could have taken younger or smaller varieties of some larger animals. Given all these factors, there was plenty of room for all the animals, food for the trip, and the eight humans aboard. — Norman L. Geisler and Thomas A. Howe, *When Critics Ask : A Popular Handbook on Bible Difficulties* (Wheaton, Ill.: Victor Books, 1992), 41–42.

13. GENESIS 6:14ff—How could a wooden ark survive such a violent flood?

PROBLEM: The ark was only made of wood and carried a heavy load of cargo. But, a world-wide flood produces violent waters that would have broken it in pieces (cf. Gen. 7:4, 11).

SOLUTION: First, the ark was made of a strong and flexible material (gopherwood) that "gives" without breaking. Second, the heavy load was an advantage that gave the ark stability. Third, naval architects inform us that a long box-shaped, floating box-car, such as the ark was, is a very stable craft in turbulent waters. Indeed, modern ocean liners follow the same basic dimensions or proportions of Noah's ark. — Norman L. Geisler and Thomas A. Howe, *When Critics Ask : A Popular Handbook on Bible Difficulties* (Wheaton, Ill.: Victor Books, 1992), 41–42.

14. GENESIS 7:24—Did the flood rains last forty days or one hundred fifty days?

PROBLEM: Genesis 7:24 (and 8:3) speak of the flood waters lasting for 150 days. But, other verses say it was only 40 days (Gen. 7:4, 12, 17). Which is correct?

SOLUTION: These numbers refer to different things. Forty days refers to how long "the rain fell" (7:12, NIV), and 150 days speaks of how long the flood "waters prevailed" (cf. 7:24).

At the end of the 150 days "the waters decreased" (8:3). After this it was not until the fifth month after the rain began that the ark rested on Mt. Ararat (8:4). Then about eleven months after the rain began, the waters dried up (7:11; 8:13). And exactly one year and ten days after the flood began, Noah and his family emerged on dry ground (7:11; 8:14). — Norman L. Geisler and Thomas A. Howe, *When Critics Ask : A Popular Handbook on Bible Difficulties* (Wheaton, Ill.: Victor Books, 1992), 41–42.

15. Back to Genesis 6.8. What does it mean to walk with God?

We read earlier that in Genesis 6, God saw how the earth was no longer the perfect paradise He purposed it to be and decided to wipe mankind from the face of the earth, because all humanity forgot Him. There was but one man and his family that still walked the walk with our heavenly Father. His name was Noah. Noah feared and wholeheartedly loved and obeyed God. Noah walked the walk in faith as a living example to his generation. And were there any benefits by way of rewards? Very much so! Noah found favour in God's eyes, in spite of, the multitude of sins he was surrounded by. — Olawunmi Biriyok, *Walk the Walk* (Maitland, FL: Xulon Press, 2013).

16. How is life different for us when we walk with God?

Walk with God as Noah did: when the flood came, Noah was saved amidst the scorn and rejection of his neighbors. Walk with God as Moses did in the solitude of the desert: when the hour of judgment fell upon Egypt, Moses was prepared to lead his people to victory.

Walk with God as David did as a shepherd boy: when he was called to rule his people, he was prepared for the task of kingship. Walk with God as Daniel and his three young friends did in the palace of Babylon's king: when the fiery furnace and the lions' den came, God was beside them and delivered them. No, God didn't always deliver His saints from adversity or even death, nor does He today. But because they had learned to trust Him in the light, they were prepared to follow Him in the darkness.

God has not promised to deliver us from trouble, but He has promised to go with us through the trouble. "Yea, though I walk through the valley of the shadow of death, I will fear no evil; for You are with me" (Psalm 23:4). — Billy Graham, *Hope for Each Day: Morning & Evening Devotions* (Nashville: Thomas Nelson, 2012).

17. What does it take to live a life walking with God?

Noah's relationship with God was priority. He knew God was responsible for his life, liberty, and happiness. Simply put, Noah walked with God. He was not distracted by the chaos of the culture or soiled by society. So, what does it mean to walk with God? Walking is a beautiful word picture because it takes one of life's most basic acts and converts it into a supernatural relationship.

Walking implicates a relationship that is not hurried, that easily communicates, and that is invigorating. When we walk with God we are not rushed. We trust Him and are patient. Yes, there are seasons of life and cycles of time when we must be very deliberate and focused. A medical emergency causes us to rush for help, but overall, as we walk with God, we take life in stride. — Boyd Bailey, *Seeking Daily the Heart of God Volume Ii* (Atlanta: Wisdom Hunters, 2013).

18. What benefits come to those who live life walking with God?

We believe that any circumstance in life has to pass through God's protection, as He holds us in His hand (see John 10:28–30). So we stay close by Him as we walk, not rushing ahead in presumption, nor lagging behind in discouragement. Walking also implies communication. It is hard to communicate when you run. There are too many distractions.

However, a walk is disarming; eye contact is limited within a safe environment. A walk with the Lord can cover trivial pursuits, heartbreaking hurt, or the dreaming of God-sized dreams. Perhaps in your regular physical exercise, you can also stretch your spiritual muscles in conversation with your Master Trainer Jesus.

Lastly, a walk with God is invigorating. You are energized and ready to scale mountains. Your spiritual blood is pumping, and your heart is healthier. Your energy level is high because your God consciousness is elevated. Walk with God and you will survive, even thrive, within the challenges of life.

Have a little walk with Jesus, and tell Him all about your problems. He walks with you slowly through the valleys and supportively up the mountains. Grace is His guide to greater heights. How is your grace walk with Jesus?

He says, "My sheep listen to my voice; I know them, and they follow me" (John 10:27). — Boyd Bailey, *Seeking Daily the Heart of God Volume Ii* (Atlanta: Wisdom Hunters, 2013).

19. What keeps some believers from walking with God?

There are a number of things included in the concept of walking with God. The Bible says that we need to walk in the Spirit (Galatians 5:16). We should walk rooted in Him (Colossians 2:6-7). We should walk humbly with Him (Micah 6:8). The book of 1 John promises us that "if we walk in the light, as he is in the light, we have fellowship with one another, and the blood of Jesus, his Son, purifies us from all sin" (v. 7, NIV). Walking with God means moving in harmony with Him, staying close to Him. This phrase "walking with God" speaks of a joint effort.

If you go into business with someone, it means pooling your resources. Maybe you both have small businesses, even competing businesses, and one day you go to that person and agree to work together. You draw up the contracts and pool your resources. He has his clients, you have your clients, and suddenly you broaden your base.

Walking with God is like going into business with God. This means that I take all of my resources, which obviously are quite limited, and say, "Lord, here is what I have to bring. I give myself to You."

Then God says, "Here is what I bring to the table. I bring My omniscience. I bring My unlimited power. I bring My grace. I bring My knowledge of the future and My perspective of the present and past. I bring all that I have."

Essentially it would be like a billionaire going into business with a homeless person. That's a pretty good deal. The homeless person will benefit because all the billionaire's resources are now at his or her disposal. But it also means that all of his or her resources (such as they are) will now be at the billionaire's disposal.

When we walk with God, He brings all He has, all He is, to the table...but He also asks us for all we are and all we have. Through all of time and eternity, we are the ones who get the better end of that arrangement! — Greg Laurie, *Daily Hope for Hurting Hearts: A Devotional* (Dana Point, CA: Kerygma Publishing—Allen David Books, 2011).

20. What prerequisites are there to walking with God? What is required?

Twice in the Genesis passage, we are simply told that "Enoch walked with God." There is no explanation or evidence of any pressure. It doesn't say here that he was pushed up against the wall by God. He just decided, when his son was born, "I'm going to start walking with God."

That's how it starts for all of us. It doesn't come in some flash in the sky or some major event. We just one day decide. We've walked our own way and done our own thing. Now it's time to start walking with God. I believe that sooner or later every one of God's children comes to a fork in the road, a place where they make the decision, "I'm either going to walk with God or I'm going to do my own thing." You may have faced a decision like that in the past—or you may be facing such a decision now. God leaves that decision to you, just as He did with Enoch. Enoch made the right decision and was promoted to the Hall of Faith—as you and I can be. — David Jeremiah, *Heroes of the Faith: Study Guide* (Nashville, TN: Thomas Nelson Publishers, 2001), 36.

21. How would you explain to a new believer how to walk with God?

There is a progression in the characters mentioned in this chapter of Hebrews. Abel worshiped God by faith. Enoch walked with God by faith. You can't walk with God until you worship God. The first calling is to learn how to worship God. When you learn how to worship God, then you can develop a walk with God. Stop trying to get people to walk with God who won't worship. If you don't love Him enough to worship, you'll never be able to walk with Him. If you can worship like Abel, then you can walk like Enoch.

Enoch walked and by faith Noah worked with God. You can't work with God until you walk with God. You can't walk with God until you worship God. If you can worship like Abel, then you can walk like Enoch. And if you walk like Enoch, then you can work like Noah. — T. D. Jakes, *Hope for Every Moment: 365 Inspirational Thoughts for Every Day of the Year* (Shippensburg, PA: Destiny Image, 2011).

22. What do you want to recall from today's conversation?

23. How can we support one another in prayer this week?

Genesis, Lesson #5
Good Questions Have Small Groups Talking
www.joshhunt.com

Email your people and ask them to do a little research on whether this was a local or worldwide flood. There are a number of interesting videos on Youtube about it.

Genesis 8:15–9:1; 11-16

OPEN
Let's each your name and what is the longest trip you have ever taken?

DIG
1. **Background. Did anyone get a chance to do any reading on the local vss. universal flood debate? What are the arguments in favor of a local flood?**

   Proponents of a local or regional flood lean on the archaeological and geological record while incorporating the biblical story. The arguments for a local flood are:

   1) "All" does not necessarily carry a universal sense—it may be used to refer to "some" or as an expression of large in number (Seely, "Noah's Flood," 293–4; Matthews, Genesis 1–11:26, 365; compare Gen 41:56–7; 2 Sam 18:8; Dan 6:25).

   2) Archaeological and geological records do not support a global, cataclysmic flood within the last 40,000 years. Seely's research suggests "the only evidence of serious

flooding in the Near East during that time period is from riverine floods ... we have no archaeological evidence for the Flood as it is described in Scripture" (Seely, "Noah's Flood," 299; compare Carol Hill, "The Noachian Flood," 181).

3) There is insufficient water available globally to cover the earth to a depth of 8,000 feet (the average height of the mountains of Ararat). If all the rainwater were to pour out upon the earth, it would only "cover the ground to an average depth of less than two inches" (Whitcomb and Morris, The Genesis Flood, 121). Even if all available groundwater is included in the flood account (compare Gen 7:11), "it would flood the earth to a depth of less than 60 feet" (Seely, "Noah's Flood," 308). — Jason C. Kuo, "Flood," ed. John D. Barry et al., *The Lexham Bible Dictionary* (Bellingham, WA: Lexham Press, 2012, 2013, 2014).

2. What are the main arguments for a global flood?

The strongest argument for a universal, global flood event comes from the Bible itself. A straightforward reading of Gen 7:19–22 indicates the writer envisioned a flood on a massive scale—covering "all the high mountains which were under the entire heaven" (Gen 7:19). Supporters of the global flood view believe these statements should be taken at face value and then explain how such a flood might have been physically possible. In addition to the biblical account, proponents of this view point to the accounts of flood stories among unrelated peoples as evidence of some major flood event in ancient times. Opponents counter that we have no way of knowing whether these flood stories all refer to the same flood, or if these accounts simply refer to a regional flood.

The physical evidence for a global flood is limited and inconclusive. Supporters of the global view appeal to evidence of flood deposits around the world and evidence from the fossil record of animals that apparently died suddenly and violently from drowning or choking. However, the evidence may not point to a single cataclysmic event; rather, the fossils and preserved animal remains may be isolated instances spread over thousands of years. — John D. Barry et al., *Faithlife Study Bible* (Bellingham, WA: Logos Bible Software, 2012).

3. On the whole, which do you find more compelling and why?

Few texts have inspired more interest than this one. It has become the source for discussion about ethics (capital punishment), theology (the Noahic Covenant), and apologetics (evidence for the flood). Of the latter, several issues have been most prominent. The first has to do with the ark's remains. Over the last 30 years much interest has been focused on photographs which seem to depict a large wooden structure buried atop Mount Ararat in Turkey. It remains to be seen whether this will ever be resolved and whether it actually is the ark. Second, there is much discussion over evidence for the flood. New data pours in seemingly by the week. Not long ago scientists discovered the remnants of a city a hundred feet or more beneath the surface of the Black Sea. It appears that this sea was not always there or not always so expansive. This would be clear evidence of a flood in ancient times. The third issue is whether the flood was local or worldwide. Proponents of a local flood only, some of whom are evangelicals, stand in sometimes vocal opposition to those who believe the flood to have been universal. Both OT and NT texts seem clearly to teach that the flood was universal (Gen. 7:19–24; 2 Pet. 3:6). But that does not mean that any one way of arguing for a universal flood, such as the catastrophist approach, for instance, is the last word on the matter. Much work remains to be done. What can be said is that the scientific evidence for a flood, even for a universal flood, is strong and growing daily. — Chad Brand, "Flood," ed. Archie England et al. with Draper Charles, *Holman Illustrated Bible Dictionary* (Nashville, TN: Holman Bible Publishers, 2003), 585.

4. Was it unfair that God would destroy the whole earth in a flood?

For over a century, Noah proclaimed the end of the world to others, extending them an opportunity to be saved from the impending destruction. He preached a message of repentance and salvation that was very similar to the message of today's gospel. It had to be a tough audience. Noah knew God and poured all his passion into doing God's work, but only his family believed.

Noah knew the truth, proclaimed it, and believed God. He tried day after day to impress upon others the truth of God's plan that he knew in his heart. People rejected God and probably rejected Noah, but despite that rejection, he never gave up. Do you have a heart for evangelism? How passionate are you about leading others to Jesus? — Shanna D. Gregor, *Legendary Leaders of the Bible: 15 Stories You Should Know* (Uhrichsville, OH: Barbour, 2011).

5. Context. How long was Moses on the ark? [I intentionally said Moses; see if anyone catches it!]

This brings us to 261 days, so that the total time of the Flood was 371 days, extending over a year. That also conforms to the statement of Scripture that the Flood was universal; it was not just the filling of a swimming pool—it certainly was more than that!

There have been other discoveries that have revealed something concerning the Flood, and I would like to pass on to you the words of Dr. J. E. Shelley who takes the position that the Flood was universal, that it covered the entire earth: "The most striking example of this is found in the case of the mammoths. These elephants are found buried in the frozen silt of the Tundra, Siberia, all over the length of the Continent of Asia, and in the North of Alaska and Canada. They are found in herds on the higher ground not bogged in marshes, hundreds of thousands in number." He goes on to say that these elephants have been examined and found to have drowned. If they had just gotten bogged down, they would have died of starvation. "The farther north one goes, the more there are, till the soil of the islands of the White Sea inside the Arctic circle consists largely of their bones mingled with those of sabre-tooth tiger, giant elk, cave bear, musk ox, and with trunks of trees and trees rooted in the soil. There are now no trees in those regions, the nearest being hundreds almost thousands of miles away. The mammoth could not eat the stunted vegetation which now grows in this region for but three months in the year, a hundred square miles of which would not keep one of them alive for a month. The food in their stomachs is pine, hawthorn branches, etc. These mammoths were buried alive in the silt when that silt was soft. They and the silt were then suddenly frozen and have never been unfrozen. For they show no signs of decomposition. Mammoth ivory has been sold on the London docks for more than a thousand years. The Natural History Museum purchased a mammoth's head and tusks from the ivory store of the London Docks. This head was absolutely fresh and was covered with its original fur."

If you doubt the universality of the Flood, here is more than enough evidence to convince you. — J. Vernon McGee, *Thru the Bible Commentary, electronic ed., vol. 1* (Nashville: Thomas Nelson, 1997), 44–45.

6. Genesis 8.1. What does it mean that God remembered Noah? Had God forgotten?

But God remembered Noah. God, of course, had not forgotten Noah! To "remember," as it is used in Scripture, is not merely to recall to mind. It is to express concern and care for someone. For example, in the postexilic period Nehemiah desired that God "remember" him and act "with favor" (Neh. 5:19; 13:31). In Genesis 19:29 God "remembered Abraham, and he brought Lot out of the catastrophe." In Genesis 30:22 God "remembered Rachel; he listened to her and opened her womb." God is gracious when he remembers his people. So again the grace of God is emphasized when the waters begin to recede to allow the earth to dry out so mankind might live once again on the land. — *Holman Old Testament Commentary – Genesis.*

7. We always want to read the Bible for application. What is the message in this story for us? What is the application?

This passage shows that in spite of the long delay God did permit a new beginning. Some of the exiles were not entirely sure whether or not God had lost patience with the nation forever and had cast them off (Lam 5:20, 22). The message of the flood story is that after even the most severe judgment comes mercy, and a new beginning would bring encouragement and hope to the exiles and be an antidote to despair. — James McKeown, *Genesis, The Two Horizons Old Testament Commentary* (Grand Rapids, MI; Cambridge, U.K.: William B. Eerdmans Publishing Company, 2008), 63.

8. Genesis 8.20. Imagine how Noah is feeling at this point in this story. How would you put it into words?

Malachi 4:2 conjures up the sheer physical joy of release after confinement, but Noah's first thought is Godward. Homage, dedication and atonement are all expressed in the burnt offerings: the new earth is to be God's, if he will have it. — Derek Kidner, *Genesis: An Introduction and Commentary, vol. 1, Tyndale Old Testament Commentaries* (Downers Grove, IL: InterVarsity Press, 1967), 100.

9. Genesis 8.21. What does it mean that this sacrifice smelled good to God?

The phrase that Yahweh 'smelled the soothing aroma' is idiomatic—it simply means that he accepted and delighted in Noah's sacrifice. It is also emphatic: the verb carries with it a cognate noun so that it literally says, 'He smelled a smell.' That is a typical Hebrew construction to add force to the expression. In addition, the term 'soothing' (literally, 'tranquil') appears to be a word-play on the name Noah ('rest'). — John D. Currid, *A Study Commentary on Genesis: Genesis 1:1–25:18, vol. 1, EP Study Commentary* (Darlington, England: Evangelical Press, n.d.), 210–211.

10. Verse 21. Does God promise there will not be any more natural disasters?

The assurance goes far beyond 21. It does not abolish disasters, but it does localize them, so that the human family may overcome them by forethought such as Joseph's and by compassion such as Paul's (2 Cor. 8:14). — Derek Kidner, *Genesis: An Introduction and Commentary, vol. 1, Tyndale Old Testament Commentaries* (Downers Grove, IL: InterVarsity Press, 1967), 101.

11. Genesis 9.2. How did animals change after the flood?

The Noahic covenant was a reiteration of much of the original Adamic covenant but now with modifications caused by man's sin and the resulting judgments. One of the clearest aspects of the original covenants was the command to multiply. Be fruitful and increase in number and fill the earth is repeated from Genesis 1:28a. But God stopped before repeating his original command: "Subdue it. Rule over the fish of the sea and the birds of the air and over every living creature that moves on the ground" (Gen. 1:28b). Now the fear and dread of you [mankind] will fall upon all the beasts of the earth and all the birds of the air, upon every creature that moves along the ground, and upon all the fish of the sea; they are given into your hands.

There was a significant change in the way animals would now respond to mankind. Before the flood the animals "came" to Noah (Gen. 7:9, 15); now they would tend to flee from him. This was a means of survival for the animals since the Lord declared that everything that lives and moves will be food for you. Just as I gave you the green plants, I now give you everything An animal diet would cause mankind to kill various creatures. To prevent the annihilation of many species, the Lord provided animals with a fear of mankind.

The declaration that the fear and dread of you will fall upon all beasts of the earth does not mean that pets and domesticated animals are a violation of God's revelation. Man has been able to overcome the natural fear of man by animals through a process of behavioral modification. The rare and surprised "wild" reaction by trained animals reminds us that animals have an innate fear of man. — *Holman Old Testament Commentary – Genesis.*

12. Genesis 9.6. How was law/ethics changed?

The second part of God's covenant with Noah is found in Genesis 9:1-7. It deals with human government, among other things, and it does not take a careful reading of the passage to see that a new set of conditions for man's life on earth is introduced in it. Previously, when Cain killed Abel, God did not kill Cain. He pronounced a curse on him and condemned him to be a wanderer on the earth. But when Cain complained that whoever would find him would kill him, God said, "Not so; if anyone kills Cain, he will suffer vengeance seven times over" (Gen. 4:15); he put a mark on him for protection. At the end of chapter 4, there is no suggestion that Lamech, who killed a young man, was even judged by God or even had to defend himself before an earthly tribunal. Now, however, God introduces the death penalty and thus indirectly establishes the human governments that are to wield it.

Why did God do this? Like his giving of the law somewhat later, it was undoubtedly to restrain man's passions. Luther said, "God establishes government and gives it the sword to hold wantonness in check, lest violence and other sins proceed without limit." But recognizing this, I wonder if there is not also something more. Let me explain.

One of sin's unpleasant consequences is the never-ending desire of the sinner to excuse himself, regardless of how guilty he and everyone else knows he is. This is true now and must have been true in these early ages of the race too. When Adam sinned he blamed Eve and indirectly God himself ("The woman you put here with me—she gave me some fruit from the tree, and I ate it," Gen. 3:12). The woman blamed the serpent ("The serpent deceived me," Gen. 3:13). I can imagine, though the Bible does not explicitly say so, that after the murder of Abel by Cain and the increased violence in the days leading up to the flood, someone must have come along with the excuse that the reason so much crime existed is that God had not given men and women the right to punish the offender. "Look at what happened when Cain killed Abel," this person might have said. "Did Cain get what he deserved? Not at all! God actually protected him. Why, if we had been allowed to make an example of Cain, if we had been allowed to put him to death, we could have nipped behavior like his in the bud. People would have been afraid to murder, and we would have been spared this misery. The violence on earth is God's fault." In view of that argument, which I am sure must have been made, it is possible that the establishment of the death penalty in Genesis 9 is actually "a test of man by human government," a test of this theory.

Is the wickedness of man due to the lack of proper threats and penalties? Can the death penalty (and other lesser penalties) end crime? God puts it to the test. He grants the power. As we know, the argument of the objector proves wrong and the problem is seen to reside, not in the lack of proper penalties, but in the incorrigible wickedness of man's heart. — *An Expositional Commentary – Genesis, Volume 1: Creation and Fall (Genesis 1-11).*

13. Verse 8. What is a covenant and why is it important?

The common Hebrew word for "covenant" is berith [1285, 1382]. A covenant is an agreement, a treaty, or a pact between parties, which both parties swear by oath to observe. Covenants that the Lord makes with people are therefore binding; he guarantees them with an oath. They usually begin with a historical statement declaring what the Lord has done for people, then add a section of stipulations for the participants of the covenant to abide by, and conclude with a series of promises telling what God will do for them. Covenants usually have a sign that serves as a perpetual reminder for both sides that the covenant is being kept. In this chapter the covenant is unconditional, God simply promising what he will do, and it is universal, for it includes all of creation. The sign of this covenant is the rainbow. — Allen Ross and John N. Oswalt, *Cornerstone Biblical Commentary: Genesis, Exodus, vol. 1* (Carol Stream, IL: Tyndale House Publishers, 2008), 78.

14. This covenant was between God and... What do we learn about God from this?

At least four times in this covenant, the Lord mentioned "every living creature." He was speaking about the animals and birds that Noah had kept safe in the ark during the Flood (v. 10). Once again, we're reminded of God's special concern for animal life.

When the Apostle John beheld the throne room of heaven, he saw four unusual "living creatures" worshiping before God's throne, each one having a different face (Rev. 4:6-7). The first had a face like a lion, the second like a calf, the third like a man, and the fourth like an eagle. These four faces parallel the four kinds of creatures with whom God made this covenant: wild beasts, cattle, humans, and birds (see Gen. 9:9-10). These creatures are represented perpetually before the throne of God, because the Lord is concerned about His creation. They remind us that all creation worships and praises the God who provides for His creatures and rejoices in their worship.[6] — *Bible Exposition Commentary (BE Series) - Old Testament*

15. What do we need to remember every time we see a rainbow?

To help His people remember His covenants, God would give them a visible sign. His covenant with Abraham was sealed with the sign of circumcision (Gen. 17:11; Rom. 4:9-12), and the Mosaic Covenant at Sinai with the sign of the weekly Sabbath (Ex. 31:16-17). God's covenant with Noah and the animal creation was sealed with the sign of the rainbow. Whenever people saw the rainbow, they would remember God's promise that no future storm would ever become a worldwide flood that would destroy humanity.

Mark Twain and his friend William Dean Howells stepped out of church just as a violent rainstorm began. Howells said, "I wonder if it will stop"; and Mark Twain replied, "It always has." He was right; it always has! Why? Because God made a covenant and He always keeps His word.

God spoke of the rainbow as though Noah and his family were familiar with it, so it must have existed before the Flood. Rainbows are caused by the sunlight filtering through the water in the air, each drop becoming a prism to release the colors hidden in the white light of the sun. Rainbows are fragile but beautiful, and nobody has to pay to see them! Their lovely colors speak to us of what Peter called "the manifold grace of God" (1 Peter 4:10). The Greek word translated "manifold" means "various, many-colored, variegated." The rainbow reminds us of God's gracious covenant and the "many-colored" grace of God. — *Bible Exposition Commentary (BE Series)*

16. What does the rainbow teach us about God? We always want to read the Bible for application. What is the application to our lives?

Let's pursue that thought. If the rainbow reminds us of God's faithfulness and grace, then why do we fret and worry? God hasn't promised that we'll never experience storms, but He has promised that the storms won't destroy us. "When you pass through the waters, I will be with you; and through the rivers, they shall not overflow you" (Isa. 43:2, nkjv). When the clouds appear and the sun is hidden, we have nothing to fear.

Let's think about the bow. A bow is an instrument of war, but God has transformed it into a picture of His grace and faithfulness, a guarantee of peace. God could certainly turn the bow of judgment upon us, because we've broken His law and deserve judgment. But He has turned the bow toward heaven and taken the punishment for us Himself! When Jesus died on the cross, it was the Just One suffering for the unjust (1 Peter 3:18) and bearing the suffering that rightfully belonged to us.

Rainbows are universal; you see them all over the world. God's many-colored grace is sufficient for the whole world and needs to be announced to the whole world. After all, God loves the world (John 3:16), and Christ died for the sins of the world (1 John 4:10, 14).

But the rainbow isn't only for us to see, for the Lord said, "I will look upon it" (Gen. 9:16). Certainly God doesn't forget His covenants with His people, but this is just another way of assuring us that we don't need to be afraid. When we look at the rainbow, we know that our Father is also looking at the rainbow; and therefore it becomes a bridge that brings us together. — *Bible Exposition Commentary (BE Series) - Old Testament*

17. Can you think of other rainbows in the Bible?

Three rainbows. Three men in Scripture saw significant rainbows. Noah saw the rainbow after the storm, just as God's people see it today. But the Prophet Ezekiel saw the rainbow in the midst of the storm when he had that remarkable vision of the wheels and the throne (Ezek. 1:28). Ezekiel also saw living creatures and each one had four faces! One was like a man, one like a lion, one like an ox, and one like an eagle—the same faces John saw (Rev. 4:6-7).

Of course, the Apostle John saw the rainbow before the storm of judgment broke loose (v. 3). In fact, John saw a complete rainbow around the throne of God! On earth, we see "in part"; but one day in heaven, we will see things fully as they really are (1 Cor. 13:12).

The personal lesson for God's people is simply this: in the storms of life, always look for the rainbow of God's covenant promise. Like John, you may see the rainbow before the storm; like Ezekiel, you may see it in the midst of the storm; or like Noah, you may have to wait until after the storm. But you will always see the rainbow of God's promise if you look by faith. That's the Old Testament version of Romans 8:28.

God's covenant with creation affects every living creature on earth. Without it, there would be no assured continuity of nature from day to day and from season to season. We would never know when the next storm was coming and whether it would be our last.

God wants us to enjoy the blessings of natural Me and spiritual life, because He "gives to us richly all things to enjoy" (1 Tim. 6:17). When you know Jesus Christ as Lord and Savior, the world of nature around you becomes much more wonderful, because the Creator has become your Father.

When in later years the American evangelist D.L. Moody talked about his conversion as a teenager, he said, "I was in a new world. The next morning the sun shone brighter and the birds sang sweeter... the old elms waved their branches for joy, and all Nature was at peace. [It] was the most delicious joy that I had ever known."

The God of creation is the god of salvation. Trust Jesus Christ and you can then truly sing, 'This is my Father's world." — *Bible Exposition Commentary (BE Series) - Old Testament*

18. Review. What do you admire about Noah?

GOD GAVE NOAH SPECIFIC DIRECTIONS for building the ark. "Use cypress wood," God directed, "and waterproof it with tar." He gave the dimensions of the ark, the number of decks, and described locations for the window and the door. Noah did what he was told. No questions asked.

God listed the birds, domestic animals, wild animals, and small animals to be brought inside the boat. He gave the number of each—seven pairs of every animal approved for eating and sacrifice, and one pair of all the others. Noah did everything exactly as God commanded. No questions asked.

When you read the account of Noah in Genesis chapters 6–9, what stands out is the businesslike way that Noah built the ark. Would such clear directions be followed today? Or would the builder ask, "Can I substitute pine for cypress? Would mortar work as well as tar? Why a window there? Wouldn't we need an extra door?"

Noah was not only a hero of faith but also an example of what it means to be an obedient, diligent worker. If you were an employer, wouldn't you jump at the chance to hire a man such as Noah? As an employee, wouldn't you find the door always open if you had the attitude and dedication of Noah? — Compiled By Barbour Staff, *The Men of the Bible*

Devotional: Insights from the Warriors, Wimps, and Wise Guys (Uhrichsville, OH: Barbour, 2015).

19. What do we learn about following God from Noah's example?

The next hero of faith cited in Hebrews 11 is Noah: "By faith Noah, being warned by God concerning events as yet unseen, in reverent fear constructed an ark for the saving of his household. By this he condemned the world and became an heir of the righteousness that comes by faith" (v. 7). God warned Noah that He was going to send a massive deluge on the earth to destroy the human race because of its sin, but He commanded Noah to make a large boat to save his family and animal species (Gen. 6). "In reverent fear," Noah set about to do exactly what God commanded.

We know that it took Noah many years to build the ark, and many Bible scholars have made the point that Noah must have been ridiculed by the people of his time. Many years ago, I heard a comedy routine in which Bill Cosby played the role of Noah. As he was building the ark in the middle of the desert, his friends would come by and ask, "Noah, what are you doing?" He would reply, "Building a boat." "Why?" "Well, because there's going to be a flood." Cosby captured the ridicule that Noah likely experienced when he gave the response of the people: "Yeah, sure."

Building an ark in a desert is certainly ludicrous in and of itself. But Noah believed God, and he was willing to be what the New Testament speaks of as a "fool for Christ" (1 Cor. 4:10). He put his confidence not in the judgments of this world but in the judgment of God. He built the ark, through which the human race survived, because he lived by faith.

The Scriptures say that Noah's activity in this regard "condemned the world" (Heb. 11:7a). His faithfulness "showed up" the faithlessness of the other people of his day. Through this faith, he "became an heir of the righteousness that comes by faith" (v. 7b). — R. C. Sproul, *What Is Faith?, vol. 8, The Crucial Questions Series* (Lake Mary, FL: Reformation Trust Publishing, 2010), 25–26.

20. How can we support one another in prayer this week?

Genesis, Lesson #6
Good Questions Have Small Groups Talking
www.joshhunt.com

Genesis 11.1 - 9

OPEN

Let's each your name and what foreign languages have you studied?

DIG

1. **Genesis 11.1. See if you can locate Shinar on a map.**

   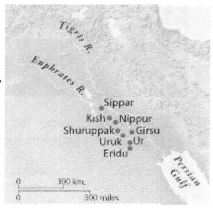

   The Hebrew term for Shinar (šin'ār) refers to the area that ancient Near Eastern texts refer to as Sumer. It covered the southern part of the Tigris-Euphrates river basin as far north as Sippar, where the rivers converge in the area of modern southern Iraq. Major cities of the region included Kish, Nippur, Shuruppak, Girsu, Uruk, Eridu, and Ur. This is the area where urbanization developed and is the heartland of Mesopotamian civilization. — John H Walton, *Zondervan Illustrated Bible Backgrounds Commentary (Old Testament): Genesis, Exodus, Leviticus, Numbers, Deuteronomy, vol. 1* (Grand Rapids, MI: Zondervan, 2009), 60.

2. Do a search for images on Tower of Babel on your smart phone. What do you imagine this looked like?

3. Did the Tower of Babel look more like the Washington Monument or the Pyramids in Egypt?

Many children's Bible stories falsely portray the Tower of Babel as a round tower, like those on a medieval castle. People mistakenly think it could be climbed until one got to heaven. The Hebrew word for tower is a "stepped ziggurat," in other words, a pyramid. It was not a tower to use in climbing to heaven, but was a religious center dedicated to the worship of heaven.

There are many archaeological remains of ziggurats in the TigrisEuphrates Valley. These pyramids were used for worship, as were the pyramids in Central and South America built by the Aztec and Inca Indians. However, the pyramids built in Egypt during this same period of history were burial vaults for Egyptian leaders. — Elmer Towns, *Bible Answers for Almost All Your Questions* (Nashville: Thomas Nelson, 2003).

4. Has the Tower ever been found?

There is considerable evidence now that the world did indeed have a single language at one time. The Sumerian literature alludes to this several times. Linguists also find this theory helpful in categorizing languages. But what of the tower and the confusion of tongues?

> It is interesting to note that Ur Nammu, King of Ur from about 2044 to 2007 B.C., supposedly received orders to build a great ziggurat (temple tower) as an act of worship to the moon god Nannat. A steel (monument) about five feet across and ten feet high shows Ur Nammu's various activities, and one panel has him setting out with a mortar basket to begin construction of the great tower. In this way he was showing his allegiance to the gods by taking his place as a humble workman. A clay tablet has been unearthed that states that the erection of the tower offended the gods, so they threw down what the men had built, scattered them abroad, and made their speech strange. This, of course, bears an interesting similarity to the record in the Bible (Gen. 11).

Norman L. Geisler and Ronald M. Brooks, *When Skeptics Ask* (Wheaton, IL: Victor Books, 1990), 184.

5. Circle every occurrence of "us" in verse 4. What do we learn about this crowd from this?

Notice that they said, "Let us build us a city ... and let us make us a name, lest we be scattered abroad." They had a bad case of perpendicular I-itis-let us make us a name! In my opinion, the sole purpose of this tower was for a rallying place for man.

The Tower of Babel was a ziggurat. There are many ruins of ziggurats in the Tigris-Euphrates Valley. I have a picture of the ruins of one in Ur of the Chaldees where Abraham lived. It was made of brick, solidly constructed, and around it was a runway which went to the top. Apparently, on top of it was an altar on which, in certain instances, human sacrifices were offered. Later on children were offered, put in a red-hot idol.

All of this was connected with the ziggurat in later history. — J. Vernon McGee, *Thru the Bible Commentary, electronic ed., vol. 1* (Nashville: Thomas Nelson, 1997), 52–53.

6. What does this tower teach us about man? What does it teach us about ourselves?

But at the time of its construction, the Tower of Babel represented the rebellion of mankind against Almighty God. Apparently it was Nimrod who led in this movement. He was the builder of the city of Babel and evidently of the Tower of Babel also. It was to be a place for him to rear a world empire that was in opposition to God.

In order to realize his ambition and to make his dreams come true, two features and factors were essential: First, he needed a center of unity, a sort of headquarters, as it were. He needed a capital, a place to assemble, a place to look to. This was why he built the city of Babel. It fulfilled one of his requirements to carry out his dream of world empire. Secondly, he needed a rallying point, not just geographical but psychological, that which gives motive—a spark, an inspiration, a song, a battle cry, sort of like a "rally-around-the-flag-boys." There had to be some impelling and compelling motivation. There had to be a monument. Lenin's tomb is where Communism meets, and in Nimrod's day it was the Tower of Babel. "Let us make us" is defiance and rebellion against God. "Let us make us a name" reveals an overweening ambition. — J. Vernon McGee, *Thru the Bible Commentary, electronic ed., vol. 1* (Nashville: Thomas Nelson, 1997), 53.

7. Can you think of other examples of people who wanted to make a name for themselves?

History demonstrates that Babylonian hearts are endemic to humanity. Centuries after the fiasco at Babel, Nebuchadnezzar strode over the ramparts of his royal palace and declared, "Is not this great Babylon, which I have built by my mighty power as a royal residence and for the glory of my majesty?" (Daniel 4:30). Centuries later when King Herod, decked out in royal livery, addressed his people, they shouted, "The voice of a god, and not of a man!" (Acts 12:22). The litany of history's Babylonian hearts roll easily from our lips. Alexander the Great. Caesar Augustus—when he died, some feared that God had died. Louis XIV, the sun king. Stalin, who encouraged those who were weary to think of him. Of course, we do not need history to understand this. We have the imperial self—our tendency to become mini-potentates—to exalt our little Babylonian hearts to the thrones of our lives. — R. Kent Hughes, *Genesis: Beginning and Blessing, Preaching the Word* (Wheaton, IL: Crossway Books, 2004), 168.

8. What does this story teach us about God?

Just as we saw in the accounts of creation, the flood, and the tower of Babel, we are seeing that God controls every aspect of the world He created, and He will not share His authority with anyone. He fights for His own glory and proves that He is the ultimate power and only true God. — Francis Chan and Mark Beuving, *Multiply: Disciples Making Disciples, First Edition* (Colorado Springs, CO: David C Cook, 2012), 179.

9. What does God do when He see arrogance?

What does God think of this? And what does he do? This is what this story is all about. And it is told with remarkable skill and care.

The literary structure of this account is another example of a perfectly balanced story in which the second half is a reversed mirror-image of the first half—an extended chiasmus. The story's central hinge is in verse 5, where the Lord comes down "to see the city and the tower, which the children of man had built." From there on the story becomes a point-for-point inversion of the first half.

A   "The whole earth had one language" (v 1)

B   "there" (v. 2)

C   "each other" (v 3)

D	"Come, let us make bricks" (v 3)
E	"let us build for ourselves" (v 4)
F	"a city and a tower"
G	"the LORD came down ... " (v 5)
F1	"the city and the tower"
E1	"which mankind had built"
D1	"come ... let us mix up" (v 7)
C1	"each other's language"
B1	"from there" (v 8)
A1	"the language of the whole earth" (v 9)

We see here: Human Arrogance (vv. 1–4), Heaven's Awareness (v. 5), and Heaven's Reversal (vv. 6–9). — R. Kent Hughes, *Genesis: Beginning and Blessing, Preaching the Word* (Wheaton, IL: Crossway Books, 2004), 168–169.

10. Besides wanting to make a name for themselves, what other sin are these people guilty of?

There is nothing inherently wrong with building a tower. In fact, it must have seemed like a great idea. After all, Babel was surely a feat of architectural beauty. And it was bringing people together in a common cause. So what could have been so wrong?

Well, we must remember Genesis 9:1, when God instructed mankind, through Noah, to "Be fruitful and multiply, and fill the earth." And again in 9:7 he told them to "Populate the earth abundantly and multiply in it." God's instructions were clear. The people were not to hunker down in one spot. They were to spread out over the whole earth! But listen to 11:1–2: "Now the whole earth used the same language and the same words. It came about as they journeyed east, that they found a plain in the land of Shinar and settled there."

What was so wrong with the tower of Babel? First, that there never should have been a Babel! There never should have been this gathering together of the earth's population in the first place. The people had done what seemed convenient instead of what was commanded! It seemed much wiser to congregate together in one large metropolis than to be "scattered abroad over the face of the whole earth" (v. 4). So they ignored God's clear instructions in favor of their own wisdom. — Kurt Strassner, *Opening up Genesis, Opening Up Commentary* (Leominster: Day One Publications, 2009), 52–53.

11. What does it mean that the Lord, "came down to see..."?

The Lord is described as coming down to see. This is a figure of speech, known as "anthropomorphic," when God is described as having a human form or attributes that belong to humans. The presence of the Lord is said to be on earth in order to obtain information. Certain theologians insinuate that this was required because God is not an all-knowing God but must seek out information. But the God of creation is an eternal, all-powerful, all-knowing God. This figure of speech is better taken as informing the readers that the transcendent God is also the imminent God who responds to man's actions. — *Holman Old Testament Commentary – Genesis.*

12. What was the tower made out of?

Stone is not readily available in the alluvial plain of southern Mesopotamia, so a logical economical choice is to use brick—there is plenty of mud. Mudbrick, however, is not durable, so it was a great technological development to discover that baking the brick made it as durable as stone. This was still an expensive process, since the kilns had to be fueled. As a result, mudbrick was used as much as possible, with baked brick used only for outer shells of important buildings or where waterproofing was desirable.259 — John H Walton, *Zondervan Illustrated Bible Backgrounds Commentary (Old Testament): Genesis, Exodus, Leviticus, Numbers, Deuteronomy, vol. 1* (Grand Rapids, MI: Zondervan, 2009), 60.

13. Was there only one language before the Tower of Babel? What was it?

When man was made in the image of God, he received God's personhood—intellect, emotion, and will. Part of that intellectual ability was the rational use of language (the ability to assign meaning to word symbols, call them to mind when necessary, and use them in communication with others). When Adam spoke with God, he used the language that God had been speaking throughout eternity, the same language the Trinity spoke among Themselves. So before the Tower of Babel, all people spoke the same language, the language of God. There were probably word derivations that different people created, though. For instance, cursing was invented by man to express his frustration or rebellion or sin.

When God changed men's languages at the Tower of Babel, it was more than changing their database of words. It probably included changing their ways of thinking, cultures, values, and the meanings they gave to words. — Elmer Towns, *Bible Answers for Almost All Your Questions* (Nashville: Thomas Nelson, 2003).

14. Besides language, what else was changed at the Tower of Babel?

Most biblical teachers feel that the various races or ethnic divisions of people happened at Babel. First, because language is more than word symbols, and conveys motives, objectives, and values that people give to words, as different groups of "language-speakers" began to develop, different cultures developed. Second, as groups of "language-speakers" migrated to various parts of the earth, they adapted to certain environmental traits, such as the darkening of the skin by long exposure to sun or the bleaching of the skin in far northern locations where there is less sun. Third, because we are products of the things we eat, and all food has its origin from the ground, the mineral differences in the geographical locations eventually produced differences in skin and hair texture, as well as in the various appearances of individuals. As an illustration, the lack of iodine in the soil in certain locations produces differences in size and skin pigmentation.

Some Bible teachers feel that the original differences in the races were embryonically in the genes of Adam when he was created, and were passed on to succeeding generations. The differences between the races were simply enhanced by environmental and mineral influences after people were scattered across the earth. God originally intended different races—therefore, we cannot attribute the differences solely to environment—because God had a divine purpose in making each different ethnic group. Each race of people manifested a certain strength from the personhood of God, and a total view of God's personhood is seen by looking at Him through all the different races. — Elmer Towns, *Bible Answers for Almost All Your Questions* (Nashville: Thomas Nelson, 2003).

15. One chapter later, God promises to make Abraham's name great—the very thing these people were trying to do. What is the difference?

There is a clear contrast between what God says here and what happened at the Tower of Babel. God says that He will make Abram's name great, in explicit contrast to Genesis 11:4, where man wanted to make his own name great.

The key difference is this: When man undertakes to make his own name great, he takes credit for his own accomplishments and does not give glory to God. But when God undertakes to make a person great, the only proper response is trust and gratitude on the part of man, which gives all glory back to God, where it belongs. Abram proved himself to be very different from the builders of the Tower of Babel because (as we see in Genesis 15:6) Abram trusted God. — John Piper, *Desiring God* (Sisters, OR: Multnomah Publishers, 2003), 310–311.

16. Did they make a name for themselves? Did they accomplish what they want?

The narrative begins with the migration of the people down to the region of Shinar, the area later known as Babylon. They settled there and began to build their city and tower to make a name for themselves. From their motive and from their actions it becomes clear that these "Shinarites" had immense pride—what one could call hubris. They had been commanded to spread out and fill the earth (9:7), but they came together and strengthened their identity. This was open rebellion against the command of God; more than that, it was independence from God. In the Bible, humility is often equated with trust and obedience, and pride with independence and disobedience. Here they came together to strengthen themselves with their building and to become famous. They were driven by the fear of being scattered and the pride of becoming famous. They tried to avoid the very thing God wanted; and the way they chose to avoid it would make them famous, but not as they thought. — Allen Ross and John N. Oswalt, *Cornerstone Biblical Commentary: Genesis, Exodus, vol. 1* (Carol Stream, IL: Tyndale House Publishers, 2008), 90.

17. How have you seen people try to make a name for themselves today?

"Let us make for ourselves a name." Isn't that the mantra of our age? It's why we wear what we wear; why we drive what we drive; why pastors long for the bigger and better church. It is why the Pharisees (like some of us) loved to do their religious deeds—to be noticed by men. Self-promotion is simply the air we breathe in the Western world. So we need constantly to ask ourselves: Am I purchasing this item/seeking this promotion/performing this service so that I might feel better about myself/attract attention to myself/live more comfortably for myself? Or am I doing it for the glory of God? — Kurt Strassner, *Opening up Genesis, Opening Up Commentary* (Leominster: Day One Publications, 2009), 54.

18. Why did God judge these people?

The narrative turns with the Lord's coming down "to look at the city and the tower the people were building" (11:5). The words of the Lord deliberately mimicked their words, "Come, let's go down and confuse" (11:7) to show that their work was going to be undone. The reason for the divine judgment on the people of Shinar is expressed in terms of the threat that their unity posed. The Lord said, "If this people, having one language, have begun to do this, then nothing they set out to do will be impossible for them" (11:6, my translation). Thus, what they would not do in obedience, God did through the judgment, and what they would have done in disobedience, God prevented by confusing and dispersing them (11:8). The work of God was preventive as well as punitive. — Allen Ross and John N. Oswalt, *Cornerstone Biblical Commentary: Genesis, Exodus, vol. 1* (Carol Stream, IL: Tyndale House Publishers, 2008), 91.

19. We always want to read the Bible for application. What is the lesson for us?

A few years ago the Arizona Republic carried this local profile by columnist E. J. Montini:

> It is dusk. Gordon Hall stands at an overlook on his 55,000-square-foot mansion in Paradise Valley, a structure built by Pittsburgh industrialist Walker McCune and now owned and being renovated by Hall. He is 32 years old and a millionaire many times over. He stares at the range of lights stretching before him from horizon to horizon and breathes a deep, relaxed sigh.
>
> The lights of the city are like the campfires of a great army to Hall, who sees himself as its benevolent general. They are like the flashlights of the world's fortune seekers, and Hall is their beacon to riches. They are, for Hall, like the stars of the firmament. And he is above them.
>
> He is worth more than $100 million, he says, because it was his goal to be worth more than $100 million before

the age of 33... There are other goals. By the time he is 38, he will be a billionaire. By the time his earthly body expires—and he is convinced he can live to be 120 years old—he will assume what he believes to be his just heavenly reward: Gordon Hall will be a god.

"We have always existed as intelligences, as spirits," he says. "We are down here to gain a body. As man is now, God once was. And as God is now, man can become. If you believe it, then your genetic makeup is to be a god. And I believe it. That is why I believe I can do anything. My genetic makeup is to be a god. My God in heaven creates worlds and universes. I believe I can do anything, too."

He looks to the horizon, and then he looks behind him, where his great dark house seems to drift like a ship in the night sky.

Gordon Hall's delusion is only another expression of humanity's primeval desire to displace God, even becoming as God himself. — R. Kent Hughes, *Genesis: Beginning and Blessing, Preaching the Word* (Wheaton, IL: Crossway Books, 2004), 167–168.

20. One lesson from this story is a reminder that God opposes the proud. Why does God hate pride so?

When Napoleon set out to conquer Russia at the head of the Grand Army of Europe, someone reminded him that "man proposes but God disposes." The conqueror of Europe replied, "I am he that both proposes and disposes." Napoleon would have fit right in as the leader of the people at Babel. But God has always resisted the proud and given grace to the humble.

C. S. Lewis wrote:

> The essential vice, the utmost evil, is Pride. Unchastity, greed, drunkenness, and all that are mere flea biters in comparison; it was through Pride that the devil

became the devil: Pride leads to every other vice: It is the complete anti-God state of mind.... As long as you are proud you cannot know God. A proud man is always looking down on things and people: and, of course, as long as you are looking down, you cannot see something that is above you (Lewis, 94, 96).

As we find ourselves in the midst of "the Great American dream," we must not develop the attitude of those whom God found so despicable at Babel. An ungodly, independent attitude, a rejection of God's mandates for humanity, a desire for earthly immortality—all these are signs that we are descendants of Babel. As we hear the languages of the world being spoken around us, we should be motivated to stay humble and true to the Lord. — *Holman Old Testament Commentary – Genesis.*

21. What good things some to those who humble themselves before God?

I always loved the movie Chariots of Fire and the story of Eric Liddell, the sprinter from Scotland who ran in the 1924 Olympics. He won a medal for his efforts, and many said his run was the "jewel of the games that year." Some great quotes came out of that movie.

One of them happened when he explained to his sister why he had to run. Because the qualifying heats for his best event, the 100-meter sprint, were held on a Sunday, he refused to participate. But he still wanted to run. He told his sister, "When I run, I feel [God's] pleasure."

When he finally ran in the 400-meter race, an event he did not excel at, one of the contestants passed him a little piece of paper. On it was written, "He who honors me, I will honor" (see 1 Samuel 2:30).

Liddell went on to win. God honored him as he had honored God. — Gary Chapman and James Stuart Bell, *Love Is a Verb Devotional: 365 Daily Inspirations to Bring Love Alive* (Grand Rapids, MI: Baker, 2011).

22. How do we humble ourselves?

Christ's command is clear to His children: "Humble yourselves." What He requires is a volitional and willful act of humility. Just like I choose to love, I choose to humble myself. I can be humble like I can be compassionate, forgiving, and gentle. Humility is not an outside force waiting to have its way; it indwells the believer waiting for action.

So how do we humble ourselves? It is submission to God and others that unleashes humility. It will lie dormant and a doormat to pride unless we surrender to our Savior Jesus. We give up our right to be right so we can walk in humility. It is taking the low place that gains the high ground of grace. Humility is the preserver of peace, while pride is the disturber of peace. We first humble ourselves and then trust God to do what is right.

Are you at enmity with the Lord? If so, humble yourself. Are you at odds with an individual? If so, humble yourself. Did you mess up at work? If so, humble yourself and take responsibility for your poor performance. Did you speak harsh and hurtful words? If so, humble yourself and ask for forgiveness. Humility heals, while pride prolongs pain.

It is the proactive process of humbling ourselves that keeps power from feeding our pride and fame from deflating our faith. Success is an enemy to humility because it tries to move us from submission to self-sufficiency. Leaders, do not let the accolades of man soften your submission to God. If you act like you do not need the Almighty, He will allow you to fall on your face in forced submission. It is better to voluntarily submit to authorities in heaven and on earth than to be made to surrender and be humiliated.

Grace is the gift you receive from God when you humble yourself. Grace is the gasoline that runs the engine of an eternal and abundant life. Humble yourself and watch the Lord lift you up in His timing. Self-exaltation is not sustainable; eternity's exaltation is forever. Submit under His mighty hand, and you will decrease, while He increases.

"He must become greater; I must become less" (John 3:30).
— Boyd Bailey, *Seeking Daily the Heart of God Volume Ii* (Atlanta: Wisdom Hunters, 2013).

23. What do you want to recall from today's study?

24. How can we support one another in prayer this week?

Genesis, Lesson #7
Good Questions Have Small Groups Talking
www.joshhunt.com

Genesis 12.1 - 9

OPEN

Let's each your name and what foreign countries you have visited.

DIG

1. Genesis 12.1 – 9. What do you learn about following God from this passage?

When you follow God, you never know where you are going. It is not like driving with an old-fashioned Rand-McNally map book where you can lay it out and see the whole thing. You can turn to state maps and city maps to see more detail. Following God is like driving with a GPS on and all you get is the voice prompts.

Sometimes, as was true with Abraham, you won't hear anything for a long time. If you have ever driven with a GPS, you will know how familiar this is. If you get on I-10 and drive across Texas, you will not hear anything for hours. Then, the voice will jar you out of your coma.

Following God is like that. You rock along—day and night, month after month, year after year—then, "turn left, go there, do this, stop doing that."

If you are addicted to certainty, you might not like following God very much. If you love detailed plans, following God might frustrate you. If you prefer the boring to the adventure of the unknown, then following God might not be your cup of tea. — Josh Hunt, Following God

2. Is following God unpredictable?

From the beginning, God's open doors meet people's closed hearts. Abram said,

> Where are these places you want me to go?
> When will I get there? How will I know?
> Will I need a design? Will I need a degree?
> Will I need other things that you're hiding from me?
> Where is the map of your plan for my life?
> I must know all this stuff. I must talk to my wife.
> I'm old. I'm not bold. And you're leaving things out.
> There are bales of details you must tell me about!

And lo! The Lord didn't tell him. The Lord is notoriously fuzzy about details like that. Knowing too many details would take all the excitement out of the adventure. God wanted Abram to be his friend, and friends trust each other, and you can't learn to trust someone without a little risk and uncertainty and vulnerability.

God told Abram, "Go to the place I will show you."

Oh, the places you'll go!

That's where the open door leads. To the place where God guides.

God opened a door. Abram went. And the rest is history.

Where will your doors lead?

John Ortberg, *All the Places You'll Go . . . except When You Don't: God Has Placed before You an Open Door. What Will You Do?* (Carol Stream, IL: Tyndale, 2015).

3. Anyone have a map? Where was Abraham coming from?

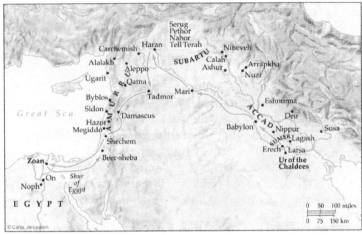

Wright, Paul H. Rose Then and Now Bible Map Atlas with Biblical Background and Culture. Torrance, CA: Rose Publishing, 2012.

4. Who can tell about a time in your life when you followed God even though you didn't know exactly how it was all going to work out?

One of the big problems with open doors is that they're not always well marked. When God does call, the call may not always be clear. As a general rule, with God, information is given on a need-to-know basis, and God decides who needs to know what, when.

A classic example of this comes in the book of Acts. The church has to decide if God is calling them to include Gentiles in a radical new way. After much prayer they send out a letter: "It seemed good to the Holy Spirit and to us . . ." (Acts 15:28).

Really? "It seemed good"? The future of the entire human race is at stake, and the best you can do is "it seemed . . ."?

And yet the church leaders were quite comfortable sending out this letter. God could have put an ad on Craigslist: "Now accepting Gentile applicants." But apparently his will for his people was that they should not be told exactly what his will was. Apparently, he knew they would grow more if they had to think and debate and argue it out than if they got a memo. And apparently, they didn't demand certainty. They were willing to settle for sincere obedience.

From the beginning of God's interactions with humanity, he seems to give information on a need-to-know basis. Ambiguity and uncertainty are woven into the story from the beginning. — John Ortberg, *All the Places You'll Go . . . except When You Don't: God Has Placed before You an Open Door. What Will You Do?* (Carol Stream, IL: Tyndale, 2015).

5. How do you feel about following God when it is sometimes unpredictable?

There is a reason why the idea of embracing uncertainty makes us uncomfortable. Modern brain science reveals that our brains are hard-wired to hate uncertainty:

> Neuroscience research is revealing that the state of not being certain is an extremely uncomfortable place for our brains to live: The greater the uncertainty, the worse the discomfort.
>
> What this tells us is that the brain doesn't merely prefer certainty over ambiguity—it craves it. Our need to be right is actually a need to "feel" right. Neurologist Robert Burton coined the term "certainty bias" to describe this feeling and how it skews our thinking.
>
> The truth for us all is that when we feel right about a decision or a belief—whether big or small—our brains are happy. Since our brains like being happy, we like feeling right. — Josh Hunt, *Following God* (Pulpit Press, 2015).

6. What place does planning have in following God?

Planning has its place. Consider these verses:

- Any enterprise is built by wise planning, becomes strong through common sense, and profits wonderfully by keeping abreast of the facts. Proverbs 24:3–4 (The Living Bible)

- Suppose one of you wants to build a tower. Won't you first sit down and estimate the cost to see if you have enough money to complete it? Luke 14:28

- The plans of the diligent lead to profit as surely as haste leads to poverty. Proverbs 21:5

- But the noble make noble plans, and by noble deeds they stand. Isaiah 32:8

- Many are the plans in a person's heart, but it is the LORD's purpose that prevails. Proverbs 19:21

- Now listen, you who say, "Today or tomorrow we will go to this or that city, spend a year there, carry on business and make money." Why, you do not even know what will happen tomorrow. What is your life? You are a mist that appears for a little while and then vanishes. Instead, you ought to say, "If it is the Lord's will, we will live and do this or that." James 4:13–15 — Josh Hunt, *Following God* (Pulpit Press, 2015).

7. What was life like for Abraham before this call?

"The Lord had said unto Abram..." When had the Lord said this? Twenty-five years previously, when Abram was approximately fifty years old. By virtue of the fact that he lived in the city of Ur—the "hot spot" of the day where bathtubs were first invented—Abram had done pretty well for himself. In addition to riches, Abram had respect, for he was a leader, with a stunningly beautiful wife. Also, Abram was religious. Joshua tells us he worshiped the moon god. Yet although he was rich, respected, and religious, Abram was also lost. He was headed for hell, until the Lord sovereignly in His mercy and grace reached down to Hot Tub City and made Himself known to Abram. — Jon Courson, *Jon Courson's Application Commentary: Volume One: Genesis–Job* (Nashville, TN: Thomas Nelson, 2005), 58.

8. Do you think there were ever moments when Abraham regretted following God?

I wonder how Noah felt, cramming his family onto a luxury animal cruise (Gen. 6:13–7:5).

Did Abraham ever regret moving from Ur to Canaan (Gen. 12:1–4)?

Or did Joseph question his forced relocation into slavery (Gen. 37:12–28)?

I wonder if Moses ever thought that moving his family and his people to the promised land was a mistake (Genesis–Deuteronomy).

I'm sure at times all of them suffered a twinge of doubt, but overall, in the end, it made sense. Why? Because God called all of them to these places.

Hebrews 11 summarizes the stories of people who were asked to do things by God, but none of the tasks made sense at the time. They acted in faith. The kind of faith that does but never sees.

If God called you to a foreign mission field, he already knows all the parameters, all the possibilities, all the problems that could occur. He's considered what will happen to you and your spouse, how it will affect your kids, and what it will mean to the people you serve.

He took care of Noah, Abraham, Joseph, Moses, and their families as they moved out into foreign mission fields.

Why not you? — Max Lucado, *Max on Life: Answers and Inspiration for Today's Questions* (Nashville: Thomas Nelson, 2011).

9. How old was Abraham when God called him?

GOD'S CALL of Abram began with an imperative —a clear command. God told him to leave his country for a land that He would show him . . . sometime later. To receive the promised blessings, Abram had to leave behind everything he relied on for safety and provision —homeland and relatives —and trust that God would honor His commitment. The call he received as a nomad for the Lord was a call to move, a call to go, a call to leave behind the comfortable and the familiar.

Put yourself in Abram's place for a moment. You're roughly seventy-five years old, with a wife in her mid-sixties. You've lived in one place your whole life. You have an established homestead in a familiar city with family and a community you've known since birth. Suddenly, the Lord appears to you in a manifestation you cannot deny as authentically supernatural, and He tells you to pack up and hit the road for an undisclosed destination.

Everything within us recoils from making big changes without thorough planning. Most of us need to see where we're jumping before committing to a leap. But God called Abram to obey this call without complete information. Abram didn't know where he was going, so he couldn't trust in a well-thought-out, long-range plan. Nevertheless, the Lord gave Abram sufficient information to make a reasonable decision.

When Abram encountered the Lord, he knew that God was real. The undeniable echo of God's voice left him no room for doubt. While his neighbors thought he had lost his mind, Abram had good reason to trust in God, even without knowing every detail of the plan. — Charles R. Swindoll, *Faith for the Journey: Daily Meditations on Courageous Trust in God* (Carol Stream, IL: Tyndale, 2014).

10. We have talked about following God, let's talk about God Himself. What do we learn about God from this passage?

Note the repetition of the word great:

> I will make you into a great nation, and I will bless you;
> I will make your name great, and you will be a blessing.
> Genesis 12:2

Imagine how you would feel if God came and said this to you: I will make you great.

I will make you a best-selling author.

I will make you a rock star.

I will make you rich.

Now, we get ourselves in trouble when these things are our idea and we insist on them. For every Billy Graham God makes there are a hundred thousand country preachers. God gets to decide.

Funny things about country preachers, though. They tend to like the country. They like walking into a restaurant and knowing everyone there. God fits us for what we were made for.

I wonder though, how many God called to the big stage and they were disobedient because they didn't think that sounded like ministry. They thought God only called people to the menial and obscure. They should re-read this passage.

Embrace God's calling on your life, big or small. If He wants you to be a rock star, be a rock star. If He wants you to sweep floors, sweep with joy. — Josh Hunt, *Following God* (Pulpit Press, 2015).

11. Are we to serve God so that we will be blessed?

Satan asked God, "Does Job serve God for nothing?"

Implication: if you serve God for reward—that is bad.

Notice it is Satan that asked this question. God is all about reward. The original covenant with Abraham emphasizes that God will bless Abraham. In Genesis 15.1 we read that God is Abraham's great reward. The promise of reward and blessing is repeated in Genesis 18.18 and 22.17. It is repeated again to Abraham's kids and grandkids.

My favorite verse teaches that you cannot come to God unless you believe that He exists (most people do) and that God is a rewarder (most people don't). (Hebrews 11.6)

God is a rewarder. God is good. It is good to follow God. It is always in our best interest to live the Christian life. It is always good for us to follow God. There is no conflict between what is good for me and what is good for God. You must believe that God is a rewarder or, according to Hebrews 11.6, you can't come to God.

I don't think this is saying God will reject you if you try to come to Him. It is just stating the nature of things—you won't try to come to God unless you believe it is good for you to do so. — Josh Hunt, *Following God* (Pulpit Press, 2015).

12. Are we to pursue holiness or happiness?

I read this in a commentary last night: If people serve God only for what they get out of it, then they are not serving God at all, they are only serving themselves by making God their servant.

It sounds good. It preaches well. It reminds me of the saying by the preacher, "God is more interested in your holiness than your happiness." As if they were separate! As if they were opposite! As if they don't come together!

Holiness and happiness come together. The happiest people on the planet are people who live holy lives. And, you can't be holy unless you are obedient to the command of a holy God to, "rejoice in the Lord always" (Philippians 3.1; 4.4) and, "Delight yourself in the Lord." (Psalm 37.4)

The writer of Hebrews said you can't come to God unless you believe He exists and that He rewards those who earnestly seek him. (Hebrews 11:6) You can't. Let that sink in. You won't. We are irrevocably hard wired to pursue what we believe to be in our best interest. We must come to love the

Christian life, or we will never come to live the Christian life.
— Josh Hunt, *Following God* (Pulpit Press, 2015).

13. Do you think we want too much from life, or settle for too little?

What I have been saying about reward—it is not just my opinion; it is the opinion of smart people. Here is how John Piper says he discovered this truth in C.S. Lewis' writing:

> Before I saw these things in the Bible, C. S. Lewis snagged me when I wasn't looking. I was standing in Vroman's Bookstore on Colorado Avenue in Pasadena, California, in the fall of 1968. I picked up a thin blue copy of Lewis's book The Weight of Glory. The first page changed my life.
>
> If there lurks in most modern minds the notion that to desire our own good and earnestly to hope for the enjoyment of it is a bad thing, I submit that this notion has crept in from Kant and the Stoics and is no part of the Christian faith. Indeed, if we consider the unblushing promises of reward and the staggering nature of the rewards promised in the Gospels, it would seem that our Lord finds our desires not too strong, but too weak. We are halfhearted creatures, fooling about with drink and sex and ambition when infinite joy is offered us, like an ignorant child who wants to go on making mud pies in a slum because he cannot imagine what is meant by the offer of a holiday at the sea. We are far too easily pleased. — Josh Hunt, *Following God* (Pulpit Press, 2015).

14. Why did God bless Abraham? Why has He blessed us so?

Why did God call Abraham? Why did He call me? Why did He call you?

Abraham was blessed to be a blessing:

> All peoples on earth will be blessed through you. Genesis 12:3

Only those with money can help those without. Only those with strength can help the weak. Only those who are healthy can help the sick.

You are blessed to be a blessing. God wants to bless your socks off. He wants to bless your socks off so that you can bless the socks off of others. You are not to be the end of the line. You are to be the Jordan River, not the Dead Sea.

God brought Joseph to a place of position and prominence. Why? So that he could be a blessing to others.

Why do you think God gave you all the stuff that He has given you? Did you know that much of the world lives on a dollar or two a day?

Why do you think God saved you, forgave you, gave you His Holy Spirit, gave you spiritual gifts, and gave you spiritual blessings?

Do you think it selfish of you to go hard after the blessed life? It is not if your motive is right. You are blessed to be a blessing. — Josh Hunt, *Following God* (Pulpit Press, 2015).

15. Genesis 12.4. What do you admire about Abraham from this verse? Think of the calling of God on other's lives in the Bible. Did they respond as Abraham did?

In the Bible, when God calls someone to do something, no one responds by saying, "I'm ready":

- Moses: "I have never been eloquent. . . . I am slow of speech and tongue" (Exodus 4:10).

- Gideon: "How can I save Israel? My clan is the weakest in Manasseh, and I am the least in my family" (Judges 6:15).

- Abraham: "Will a son be born to a man a hundred years old?" (Genesis 17:17).

- Jeremiah: "Alas, Sovereign LORD, . . . I am too young" (Jeremiah 1:6).

- Isaiah: "Woe to me . . . for I am a man of unclean lips" (Isaiah 6:5).

- Esther: "For any man or woman who approaches the king . . . without being summoned the king has but one law: that they be put to death" (Esther 4:11).

- Rich Young Ruler: "He went away sad, because he had great wealth" (Matthew 19:22).

- Ruth: "There was a famine in the land" (Ruth 1:1).

- Saul: (Samuel was going to anoint Saul king; the people couldn't find him and asked if he was present.) "The LORD said, 'See, he has hidden himself among the baggage'" (1 Samuel 10:22, NRSV).

Too inarticulate, too weak, too old, too young, too sinful, too dangerous, too rich, too poor, too much baggage —no one ever says, "Okay, Lord —I feel ready." And God says to us what he has always said, what Jesus said to his disciples: "Ready or not . . ." — John Ortberg, *All the Places You'll Go . . . except When You Don't: God Has Placed before You an Open Door. What Will You Do?* (Carol Stream, IL: Tyndale, 2015).

16. How long did Abraham wait before he got moving?

The only time you can follow God is now. Follow God now. When He says, "jump" you say, "how high"—while you are jumping. He is God, we are not. He is Boss, we are servants.

Many think they are willing followers of Christ because they tell themselves they are willing to follow. . . tomorrow. But, tomorrow never comes. In the words of Denis Waitley, we live on "Someday Isle." To follow God, we must always follow Him now.

Here are a couple of great quotes I found on this:

- One step forward in obedience is worth years of study about it. — Oswald Chambers, quoted in Our Daily Bread, March 4, 1993

- Dr. B. J. Miller once said, "It is a great deal easier to do that which God gives us to do, no matter how hard it is, than to face the responsibilities of not doing it." — MBI's Today In The Word, November, 1989, p.11

- The cost of obedience is nothing compared with the cost of disobedience. – Anonymous

— Josh Hunt, *Following God* (Pulpit Press, 2015).

17. If Abraham were looking for excuses, what excuses could he have found for not going?

Do you ever feel past your prime? Do you ever feel your time has passed? Ever feel you are too old to do anything significant for God? Don't miss this line:

> Abram was seventy-five years old when he set out from Harran. Genesis 12:4

Seventy-five when he set out. Seventy-five and just getting started. Of course, if you are looking for an excuse, you can always find one:

- Moses stuttered.

- David's armor didn't fit.

- John Mark was rejected by Paul.

- Timothy had ulcers.

- Hosea's wife was a prostitute.

- Amos' only training was in the school of fig-tree pruning.

- Jacob was a liar.

- David had an affair.

- Solomon was too rich.

- Jesus was too poor.

- Abraham was too old.
- David was too young.
- Peter was afraid of death.
- Lazarus was dead.
- John was self-righteous.
- Naomi was a widow.
- Paul was a murderer.
- So was Moses.
- Jonah ran from God.
- Miriam was a gossip.
- Gideon and Thomas both doubted.
- Jeremiah was depressed and suicidal.
- Elijah was burned out.
- John the Baptist was a loudmouth.
- Martha was a worry-wart.
- Mary was lazy.
- Samson had long hair.
- Noah got drunk.
- Did I mention that Moses had a short fuse?

Josh Hunt, *Following God* (Pulpit Press, 2015).

18. Abraham was a man of faith. What do we learn about faith from this passage?

Hannah Whitall Smith once wrote, "Sight is not faith, and hearing is not faith, neither is feeling faith; but believing when we neither see, hear, nor feel is faith. . . . Therefore, we must believe before we feel, and often against our feelings if we would honor God by our faith."

As you read the account of Abram's life, you realize he was a man of extreme faith. God asked him to do something many would find difficult, and that was to leave his family and friends and go to an unfamiliar land.

Yet God's reassuring words in Genesis 12:2–3 lessened Abram's fear.

Abram—or Abraham, as he was later called by God—gave little thought to the fact that his name would be made great. The most important thing to him was the exercise of his faith through obedience.

When God calls you to move in a certain direction by faith, He will provide you reassurance. Your responsibility is to obey and follow Him. Abram left everything because he heard God say, "Go." Are you willing to do the same? Pray that your response to the Lord is always one of faith, love, and obedience. That way you will never miss a single blessing. — Charles Stanley, *I Lift up My Soul: Devotions to Start Your Day with God* (Nashville: Thomas Nelson, 2010).

19. What do you want to recall from today's discussion?

20. How can we support one another in prayer this week?

21. Could Rebekah have known how important her actions were?

Little did Rebekah know that doing a humble task for a stranger would make her the bride of a wealthy man who was in a covenant relationship with God. She would become the mother of Jacob, and he would become the father of the twelve tribes of Israel! Years ago, I read a quotation from a writer identified only as "Marsden," and it has stuck with me: "Make every occasion a great occasion, for you can never tell when someone may be taking your measure for a larger place." — Warren W. Wiersbe, *Be Obedient, "Be" Commentary* Series (Wheaton, IL: Victor Books, 1991), 119–120.

22. What do you want to recall from today's study?

23. How can we support one another in prayer this week?

Genesis, Lesson #8
Good Questions Have Small Groups Talking
www.joshhunt.com

Email your people and ask them to take a look at the stars in the night sky. Try to imagine how Abraham felt as he looked at the stars.

Genesis 15.1 - 16

OPEN
Let's each your name and what was one thing you were afraid of as a child?

DIG
1. **Context. How old was Abraham at this time. What do you remember of this life up to this point?**

   Abram was now apparently about eighty-five years old. He had been fourteen years in Palestine, and had, for the only time in his life, quite recently been driven to have recourse to arms against a formidable league of northern kings, whom, after a swift forced march from the extreme south to the extreme north of the land, he had defeated. He might well fear attack from their overwhelmingly superior forces. So this vision, like all God's words, fits closely to moments' needs, but is also for all time and all men. — Alexander MacLaren, *Expositions of Holy Scripture: Genesis* (Bellingham, WA: Logos Bible Software, 2009), 111.

2. How would you guess Abraham is feeling about life at this point?

Now, in the aftermath, Abram's great heart slows and spasms with doubt and fear. This is not uncommon to human experience following strenuous victories. Elijah suffered similar effects after his victory over the priests of Baal at Mt. Carmel, even fleeing to the wilderness and asking God to let him die (cf. 1 Kings 18, 19). Abram was tired, fearful, and despondent. Humanly, Abram had reasons to fear reprisals from the eastern coalition. Bigger armies might return.

Abram also had plenty of time for reflection in the postbellum quiet—his great victory had not brought him any nearer his promised inheritance. Long ago when he first responded to God's call, Sarah was barren (cf. 11:30). Their journey had begun in barrenness, but with hope in God's promise. But the thousand-mile journey, the sojourn in Canaan, the fiasco in Egypt, the return to Canaan, and the victory over the kings were all carried out under the shadow of barrenness. Now barrenness persisted. Abramservants had children. Other men's children clung to his garments. Likely, Abram mused, "So what if everybody knows my name from the Nile to the Euphrates? So what if I'm rich? What difference does it make if I have no children?" Restless, dark doubt gripped his faltering heart. Fearless Abram feared. — R. Kent Hughes, *Genesis: Beginning and Blessing, Preaching the Word* (Wheaton, IL: Crossway Books, 2004), 222–223.

3. Genesis 15.1. What does "vision" mean in this context? Have you ever had a vision?

Visions may be either visual or auditory and are not the same as dreams in that one does not have to be asleep to experience a vision. God used visions to communicate to people; they constitute a more aggressive form of communication than dreams. In contrast to this one, visions in the Old Testament were typically given to prophets in order to communicate oracles to be delivered to the people. They may involve natural or supernatural settings, and the individual having the vision may be either an observer or a participant.

Besides the category of "dream" in the ancient Near East, there are "waking dreams," but these are the dreams one has when half awake in the morning, not like biblical visions. The closest thing to biblical visions are the oracular decisions seen when a person was in a semicomatose state or trance.342 The idea of "seeing an oracular decision" makes sense both in the context of Genesis 15 (where Abram asks an oracular question, 15:8) and in the context of the prophets (where oracles emerge from the vision). As in the Old Testament, these visions are distinct from dreams but can be communicated in dreams. — John H Walton, *Zondervan Illustrated Bible Backgrounds Commentary (Old Testament): Genesis, Exodus, Leviticus, Numbers, Deuteronomy, vol. 1* (Grand Rapids, MI: Zondervan, 2009), 84.

4. Why do you think God told Abraham to fear not?

When fear dominates our life everything gets out of perspective; everything gets distorted. Ten of the twelve spies who returned to Kadesh Barnea brought back a totally distorted picture of what the Promised Land was really like. Their skewed report is found in verses 27–28. They came back and reported that the Promised Land was filled with Anakim, or giants. There were giants in the land of Canaan in those days (remember Goliath?), but not every person in Canaan was a giant. Their fear caused them to see one thing and report another. They saw great cities which were well fortified and concluded that they would never be able to take them. In fact, their fear so totally distorted their thinking that they concluded the only reason God had led them to Canaan was to destroy them!

You may think, "That is the most irrational thought you could ever have of God!" But when fear begins to control your life, you don't think correctly; rationality goes out the window. If you choose to let fear control your thinking, you will have a distorted view of the situation you are in and life in general. Everything will be totally out of perspective. You will think God has brought you into a terrible situation just to do you harm. — David Jeremiah, *Facing the Giants in Your Life: Study Guide* (Nashville, TN: Thomas Nelson Publishers, 2001), 11.

5. Take a guess—how many times do you think the phrase "fear not" appears in the Bible?

For years, I yearned for deliverance from my fears — but I wanted something more than the Lord's simple instructions to keep my eyes on him. "Why won't you just take this fear from me?" I demanded.

God in his tender mercy sent me back to his Word. There I read that perfect love casts out fear. I realized that fear will not get us through danger. But love can. God's love resides in us, but we're not always confident of that because we can't see it. We do see the dangers — being too high off the ground, perhaps, or staring into the cold face of an enemy. So we doubt, we question — and we let fear take over.

God knew that we would be afraid. That's why he tells us again and again in the Bible, "Fear not." Three hundred and fifty times he tells us. Fear not. Fear not. Fear not. Fear not. When angels appeared to characters in the Bible, the first words they spoke were usually, "Fear not."

It's like a mother instinctively reaching for her child who is crying in the storm, wrapping her arms around the trembling heart, and soothing over and over, "It's okay. I'm here with you. Don't be afraid." — Christine Caine, *Living Life Undaunted: 365 Readings and Reflections from Christine Caine* (Grand Rapids, MI: Zondervan, 2014).

6. What bad things happen to those who fear?

Fear, it seems, has taken a hundred-year lease on the building next-door and set up shop. Oversize and rude, fear is unwilling to share the heart with happiness. Happiness complies. Do you ever see the two together? Can one be happy and afraid at the same time? Clear thinking and afraid? Confident and afraid? Merciful and afraid? No. Fear is the big bully in the high school hallway: brash, loud, and unproductive. For all the noise fear makes and room it takes, fear does little good.

Fear never wrote a symphony or poem, negotiated a peace treaty, or cured a disease. Fear never pulled a family out of poverty or a country out of bigotry. Fear never saved a marriage or a business. Courage did that. Faith did that. People who refused to consult or cower to their timidities did that. But fear itself? Fear herds us into a prison and slams the doors.

Wouldn't it be great to walk out? — Max Lucado, *Imagine Your Life without Fear* (Nashville: Thomas Nelson, 2009).

7. What do people fear today? Let's make a long list.

Fear, it seems, has taken a hundred-year lease on the building next-door and set up shop. Oversize and rude, fear is unwilling to share the heart with happiness. Happiness complies. Do you ever see the two together? Can one be happy and afraid at the same time? Clear thinking and afraid? Confident and afraid? Merciful and afraid? No. Fear is the big bully in the high school hallway: brash, loud, and unproductive. For all the noise fear makes and room it takes, fear does little good.

Fear never wrote a symphony or poem, negotiated a peace treaty, or cured a disease. Fear never pulled a family out of poverty or a country out of bigotry. Fear never saved a marriage or a business. Courage did that. Faith did that. People who refused to consult or cower to their timidities did that. But fear itself? Fear herds us into a prison and slams the doors.

Wouldn't it be great to walk out? — Max Lucado, *Imagine Your Life without Fear* (Nashville: Thomas Nelson, 2009).

8. Do you think we have more to fear, or less to fear than in generations past?

And then there's the matter of basic facts. Here are a few to consider the next time someone claims with great certainty that the sky is crashing. In England, a baby born in 1900 had a life expectancy of forty-six years. Her great-grandchild, born in 1980, could look forward to seventy-four years of life. And the great-great-grandchild, born in 2003, can count on almost eight decades on the planet. The story is the same in every other Western country. In the United States, life expectancy was fifty-nine years in 1930. Seven decades later, it was almost seventy-eight years. In Canada, life expectancy recently inched above eighty years. For most of the history of our species, giving birth was one of the most dangerous things a woman could do. It is still a risky venture in much of the developing world, where 440 women die giving birth for every 100,000 children delivered. But in the developed world, that rate has plummeted to 20—and we no longer think of birth and death as constant companions. As for mothers, so for children. The experience of lowering a toddler-size coffin into the earth was painfully common not so long ago, but the odds that a baby born today will live to blow out five candles on a birthday cake have improved spectacularly. In the United Kingdom in 1900, 14 percent of all babies and young children died; by 1997, that number had fallen to 0.58 percent. Since 1970 alone, the death rate among American children under five fell by more than two-thirds. In Germany, it dropped by three-quarters. And we're not just living longer. We're living better. In studies across Europe and the United States, researchers have determined that fewer people develop chronic illnesses like heart disease, lung disease, and arthritis; that those who do develop them ten to twenty-five years later in life than they used to; and that these illnesses are less severe when they strike. People are less physically disabled than ever. And they're bigger. The average American man is three inches taller and fifty pounds heavier than his ancestor of a century ago, which makes it difficult for Civil War re-enactors, who use only authentic kit, to fit in army tents. We're even getting smarter: IQs have been improving steadily for decades.

The trends in humanity's political arrangements are also quite positive, despite what we read in newspaper headlines. In 1950, there were twenty-two full democracies. At the century's end, there were 120, and almost two-thirds of the people in the world could cast a meaningful ballot. As for the bloodshed and chaos that many people claim to see rising all around us, it just isn't so. "War between countries is much less likely than ever and civil war is less likely than at any time since 1960," Monty Marshall of George Mason University told The New York Times in 2005. A major study released later that year by the Human Security Centre at the University of British Columbia confirmed and expanded on that happy conclusion. It is well known that those of us blessed to live in Western countries are the most prosperous humans in the history of the species, but we feel a little guilty even mentioning it because we know so many others don't share our good fortune. Not so well known, however, is that there have been major improvements in the developing world, too. In the two decades following 1980, the proportion of people in the developing world who were malnourished fell from 28 percent to 17 percent. That's still unconscionably high, but it's a lot better than it was. Then there's the United Nations Human Development Index (HDI). It's probably the best measure of the state of humanity because it combines key data on income, health, and literacy. At the bottom of the HDI list of 177 countries is the African country of Niger—and yet Niger's 2003 HDI score is 17 percent higher than it was in 1975. The same trend can be seen in almost all very poor countries. Mali is 31 percent better off. Chad is up 22 percent. Doom-mongers like to point to the soaring populations of the poor world as a potential source of future catastrophe, but what the doomsters never mention is that those populations aren't soaring because women are having far more babies than in the past. It's that their babies are far less likely to die than in the past—which everybody but the grumpiest Malthusian would consider to be very good news. Put all these numbers together and what do they add up to? In a sentence: We are the healthiest, wealthiest, and longest-lived people in history. And we are increasingly afraid. This is one of the great paradoxes of our time. — *The Science of Fear: How the Culture of Fear Manipulates Your Brain* by Daniel Gardner

9. Fear is bad. We are told not to fear. Yes, but how? How can we fear less than we do?

The secret of victory over fear is faith in God. There is no problem too great for God to solve, no burden too heavy for God to carry, no battle too overwhelming for God to fight and win. God is big enough to conquer the enemies that rob us of our peace and leave paralyzing fears behind. Isaiah 12:2 doesn't say, "When I am afraid, I will trust"; it says, "I will trust, and not be afraid." Faith is not simply medicine to kill the disease; faith is spiritual power to keep us from being infected in the first place.

Notice what the prophet puts first: "Behold, God is my salvation." If you want to overcome fear, get your eyes off yourself and your feelings, and off the problems that have upset you, and get your eyes on God. The Jewish spies in the Old Testament became frightened when they investigated the Promised Land, because they saw giants and high walls and felt like grasshoppers in comparison. The enemy soldiers were big, and the walls were high, but God was far above all of them. Had the spies lifted their eyes just a bit higher and seen God, they would not have been afraid. So the first step in overcoming fear is to look by faith at God. Worship God, get a fresh glimpse of His greatness and glory, and realize that He is still on the throne. The second step is to lay hold of God's Word. Faith comes by hearing, and hearing by the Word of God. When you read the Bible, you find your faith growing. You discover that God has always been adequate for the needs of His people. — Warren W. Wiersbe, *The Bumps Are What You Climb On: Encouragement for Difficult Days* (Grand Rapids, MI: Baker Books, 2002), 97.

10. What does it mean that God is our shield? What do we learn about God from this? What is the application?

Abraham's initial concern was a fear of retaliation. But God promised him He would be his shield against armed warriors.

This is a beautiful Old Testament example of what Paul had in mind when he encouraged the Ephesians to "put on the full armor of God," so that they could take their "stand against the devil's schemes" (Eph. 6:11). — Gene A. Getz, *Men of Character: Abraham* (Nashville: B&H, 1996).

11. What does it mean that God was his very great reward?

Abraham's second concern involved his potential poverty. He had just turned down a bountiful reward from the king of Sodom, saying, "I will accept nothing" (Gen. 14:24). Once again, we see God's reassuring words, a restatement of His promise to Abraham that he would be rewarded abundantly for his faithfulness. — Gene A. Getz, *Men of Character: Abraham* (Nashville: B&H, 1996).

12. Verse 2. Paraphrase Abraham's response to God. What is Abraham feeling as he speaks to God?

The phrase O Sovereign Lord is unusual because it brings together two of God's names: Adonai and Yahweh—Master and Lord. This helps soften Abram's challenging yet reasonable question. He says to God, in so many words, "You keep promising blessings, but I'm closer to death than ever before, and I have no blood heir to receive Your covenant promises. Sarai can't get pregnant now, so exactly what reward do You mean?" Abram, trying to make sense of the Lord's promise, theorizes that perhaps his chief of staff, Eliezer, might be the heir God had in mind. That would have been the custom of his culture. — Charles R. Swindoll, *Abraham: One Nomad's Amazing Journey of Faith* (Carol Stream, IL: Tyndale, 2014).

13. Verse 5. How did this night change Abraham? What is the lesson for us?

Most people who are dissatisfied and discouraged feel that way because they haven't grasped a vision for themselves. As a leader you can help others discover their dreams and then get moving.

You may already recognize much of the potential of the people you're leading, but you need to know more about them. To help them recognize the destination they will be striving for, you need to know what really matters to them. To do that, find out these things:

What do they cry about? To know where people truly want to go, you've got to know what touches their hearts.

What do they sing about? In the long run, people need to focus a lot of energy on what gives them joy.

What do they dream about? If you can help people discover their dreams and truly believe in them, you can help them become who they were designed to be. — *Becoming a Person of Influence* / John C. Maxwell, *Leadership Promises for Every Day* (Nashville: Thomas Nelson, 2003).

14. Verse 6 is a classic. How would you explain this to someone who had not heard it before?

Five times in six verses Paul uses the word credit. The term is common in the financial world. To credit an account is to make a deposit. If I credit your account then I either increase your balance or lower your debt.

Wouldn't it be nice if someone credited your charge-card account? All month long you rrack-rrack up the bills, dreading the day the statement comes in the mail. When it comes you leave it on your desk for a few days, not wanting to see how much you owe. Finally, you force yourself to open the envelope. With one eye closed and the other open, you peek at the number. What you read causes the other eye to pop open. "A zero balance!"

There must be a mistake, so you call the bank that issued the card. "Yes," the bank manager explains, "your account is paid in full. A Mr. Max Lucado sent us a check to cover your debt."

You can't believe your ears. "How do you know his check is good?"

"Oh, there is no doubt. Mr. Lucado has been paying off people's debts for years."

By the way, I'd love to do that for you, but don't get your hopes up. I have a few bills of my own. But Jesus would love to, and he can! He has no personal debt at all. And, what's more, he has been doing it for years. For proof Paul reaches into the two-thousand-year-old file marked "Abram of Ur" and pulls out a statement. The statement has its share of charges. Abram was far from perfect. There were times when he trusted the Egyptians before he trusted God. He even lied, telling Pharaoh that his wife was his sister. But Abram made one decision that changed his eternal life: "He trusted God to set him right instead of trying to be right on his own" (Rom. 4:3 msg).

Here is a man justified by faith before his circumcision (v. 10), before the law (v. 13), before Moses and the Ten Commandments. Here is a man justified by faith before the cross! The sin-covering blood of Calvary extends as far into the past as it does into the future. — Max Lucado, *In the Grip of Grace* (Dallas, TX: Word Pub., 1996), 83–84.

15. Did Abraham suddenly become sinless?

At this point in the story, the narrator inserts a simple comment. This one-sentence aside is, in fact, one of the most significant verses in the Bible. God declared Abram righteous (see Genesis 15:6). The Hebrew word means "conformity to an ethical or moral standard." It is used to describe God's morally perfect nature in Psalm 145:17: "The LORD is righteous in all His ways and kind in all His deeds" (NASB).

Abram did not suddenly become a morally flawless person. Far from it! Later in the story, Abram sinned in spectacular fashion. Nor did his behavior suddenly conform to God's perfect standard. Nothing inherent about Abram changed at all. God declared him righteous. God, acting as the supreme Judge, applied all the rights and privileges of righteousness to Abram despite Abram's own inability to be righteous. The Lord did this because of Abram's faith. God said to him, in effect, "Give Me your spiritual checkbook." And He wrote in the credit column, "Deposited to Abram's moral account: My perfect righteousness." — Charles R. Swindoll, *Abraham: One Nomad's Amazing Journey of Faith* (Carol Stream, IL: Tyndale, 2014).

16. 2 Corinthians 5.21 declares that we too are righteous. Repeat it together: "I am righteous." Is that how you see yourself? Should you see yourself as righteous?

Since we cannot remedy our sinful state or eternal destiny through any actions of our own, we must trust in God's provision for salvation: the person and work of Jesus Christ. When Jesus died on the cross, He bore our sins, paying our sin debt in full through the sacrificial offering of His body. The Father's wrath and punishment for our sin were placed squarely on His Son.

That is the biblical doctrine of justification: Jesus Christ dying on our behalf and rising again to remove our guilt and acquit us before the bar of God's holy justice. We can now be reconciled to God through Christ's substitutionary, atoning death. But we are not justified automatically. Rather, each of us must personally accept salvation by faith, receive the gift, and—not intellectually, but volitionally—trust in Christ.

When you, by grace through faith, believe in Christ as your Savior from sin, a supernatural change of condition occurs. At the moment of your salvation, the very righteousness of God—His holy, moral character—is imparted to you. Christ instantly and permanently transforms your sinful state.
— Charles F. Stanley, *Enter His Gates: A Daily Devotional* (Nashville: Thomas Nelson Publishers, 1998).

17. What does it mean that Jesus became sin? Did Jesus become a sinner?

At noon, darkness suddenly fell on the earth. Piercing through that darkness was the fourth statement of Christ as He cried out, "'Eli, Eli, lama sabachthani?' that is, 'My God, My God, why have You forsaken Me?'" (Matt. 27:46; see also Mark 15:34).

No fiction writer would have his hero say words like these. They surprise us, disarm us, and cause us to wonder what He meant.

We are looking at something that in many ways is impossible for us as humans to fathom.

Clearly we are treading on holy ground examining such a subject, yet the impact on our lives is so significant, it certainly bears looking into. To Him was imputed the guilt of our sins, and He was suffering the punishment for those sins on our behalf. In some mysterious way that we can never fully comprehend, during those awful hours on the cross, the Father was pouring out the full measure of His wrath against sin. And the recipient of that wrath was God's own beloved Son!

God was punishing Jesus, as if He had personally committed every wicked deed committed by every wicked sinner. And in doing so He could forgive and treat those redeemed ones as if they had lived Christ's perfect life of righteousness.

Jesus accomplished in six hours what would have taken us the rest of eternity to never complete: the forgiveness of our sins! — Greg Laurie, *Finding Hope in the Last Words of Jesus* (Grand Rapids, MI: Baker, 2009).

18. What if we don't feel like the righteousness of God? What are we to do then?

What will it take to bring you to such a defining moment? Do I make light of your sin? Not for a moment. Your sin and mine nailed Jesus to that cross. Our sin separated even the Son of God from intimate fellowship with the Father. Our failure and our shame drove spikes into His hands and feet. Your shame and mine cost Jesus His life. Yet the Scriptures proclaim, "He made Him who knew no sin to be sin on our behalf, so that we might become the righteousness of God in Him" (2 Corinthians 5:21).

In other words, He took our place on that blest cross! In that blest sepulcher! Let's face it, there are and there will be moments in our lives when we get "caught in the very act." It may not be adultery but something else. It's sin just the same. But because of Jesus we don't have to live a life of self-condemnation and debilitating shame. The Savior's words to you in your tough stuff of shame are the same now as they were then: "I do not condemn you either. Go. From now on sin no more." That means you're free.

If you're reading this and feeling the weight of your own shameful past or stubborn sinful ways, I invite you to come to the Savior. He's the only One perfectly qualified to judge you and condemn you, but because of what His death accomplished, He is ready to forgive and to set you free. His invitation to freedom requires your response. It isn't automatic. Being delivered from shame's shackles necessitates your coming to the precipice of the cross and acknowledging your need for Jesus. He will be there to cleanse you and make you whole.

Are you tired? Worn out? Burned out on religion? Come to me. Get away with me and you'll recover your life. I'll show you how to take a real rest. Walk with me and work with me—watch how I do it. Learn the unforced rhythms of grace. I won't lay anything heavy or ill-fitting on you. Keep company with me and you'll learn to live freely and lightly. (Matthew 11:28–30 MSG) — Charles R. Swindoll, *Getting through the Tough Stuff: It's Always Something!* (Nashville: Thomas Nelson, 2004).

19. What do you want to recall from today's conversation?

20. How can we support one another in prayer this week?

Genesis, Lesson #9
Good Questions Have Small Groups Talking
www.joshhunt.com

Genesis 17

OPEN

Let's each your name and how old are your parents—or, how old were they when they died?

DIG

1. **Context. What going on in Abraham's life? What do you remember about his life up to this point?**

    Thirteen years passed between the end of chapter 16 and the beginning of chapter 17. Ishmael was now a teenager, and Abram received a visit from El-Shaddai, the Almighty. This was God's special name for confrontation with the patriarchs. God asked Abram to continue walking in righteousness and confirmed the covenant of the seed. This chapter raises Abram to a new level of spiritual experience. Apparently his continuing need for confidence and reassurance occasioned this fresh revelation from God. — *Holman Old Testament Commentary – Genesis.*

2. **We tend to think of a day in the life of an Old Testament character as a miracle a day. Is this how it was?**

    THIRTEEN YEARS passed, and Abram didn't hear anything from God. There was no vision. There was no voice. There was no visit. Only silence. Try to imagine: complete silence on God's part for thirteen years.

Abram hadn't handled the Lord's earlier silence very well. After God's first appearance in Ur, Abram had been talking rather regularly with Him. More than once, the Lord had appeared to Abram with reassurances. Around his seventy-ninth birthday, he'd met with God after a miraculous victory on the battlefield, but then he heard nothing for another six or seven years. Then when he was eighty-five, he and Sarai decided to implement their own plan.

When his decision to run ahead of God's plan ended in spectacular failure, Abram came to a kind of end. As the expression goes, "he finally came to the end of himself." While his longing for God's promise remained front and center in his mind, he at last surrendered to God's omniscient, sovereign care.

In this next encounter with God, Abram posed no questions and made no complaints about his long wait; he merely "fell on his face" (Genesis 17:3, NASB) before his divine Friend.

After thirteen years, the Lord broke the silence with a fresh reintroduction. When He appeared to Abram, He said, "I am El-Shaddai" (Genesis 17:1). A good paraphrase would be, "I am God . . . specifically, the almighty One." — Charles R. Swindoll, *Faith for the Journey: Daily Meditations on Courageous Trust in God* (Carol Stream, IL: Tyndale, 2014).

3. Overview. Circle every occurrence of the word "covenant" in this passage.

The phrase "My covenant" is used nine times in this chapter and defines God's relationship with Abraham. This was not another covenant, different from the one God had already established with Abraham (Gen. 12:1-3; 15:1-21). It was a reaffirmation of that covenant, with the important addition of circumcision, the sign and seal of the covenant.

God promised once again to multiply Abraham's family, even though he and his wife did not have any children. His descendants would be "as the dust of the earth" (13:16) and as the stars of the heavens (15:5). These two comparisons—earth and heaven—suggest that Abraham would have a

physical family, the Jews (Matt. 3:9), and a spiritual family made up of all who believe in Jesus Christ (Gal. 3:26-29).
— *Old Testament - The Bible Exposition Commentary – Pentateuch.*

4. Verse 1. How does God introduce Himself?

Thirteen years pass in silence while Abram waited for the fulfillment of the promise. The Lord appears to Abram with time running out on the promise. He is 99 years old and Sarai 89. While the narrator calls him the Lord, he actually introduces himself as God Almighty (אֵל שַׁדַּי, ʾēl šadday). Abram apparently needed to be reminded of God's power since he had been trying to give assistance to the all powerful who had no need of it. Instead of trying to play God, Abram is commanded to "walk" before the Lord. This verb הָלַךְ (hālak, "to walk") is used in the hithpael in instances where the Lord is, or is to be, especially near. The Lord "walked" in the Garden in the cool of the day (Gen 3:8); Enoch and Noah were said to have walked with God (Gen 5:22, 24; 6:8). The Lord's presence in the Tabernacle or Temple is often indicated by reference to his walking in the hithpael (1 Sam 2:30, 35; 2 Sam 7:6-7; 1 Chr 17:6). Here Abram is commanded to "walk before" the Lord. In Genesis 24:40 the aged Abraham tells his servant that he has, in fact, been walking before the Lord. — *The College Press NIV Commentary – Genesis, Volume 2.*

5. Why do you suppose God introduces Himself as El Shaddai at this point in the story?

The Hebrew name is "El Shaddai" (shuh-DYE), and this is the first time it occurs in Scripture. "Shaddai" is translated as "Almighty" forty-eight times in the Old Testament. In the New Testament, the Greek equivalent is used in 2 Corinthians 6:18 and Revelation 1:8; 4:8; 11:17; 15:3; 16:7 and 14; 19:6 and 15; and 21:22. It is translated "Almighty" except in Revelation 19:6 ("omnipotent").

"El" is the name of God that speaks of power; but what does "Shaddai" mean? Scholars do not agree. Some say it comes from a Hebrew word meaning "to be strong"; others prefer a word meaning "mountain" or "breast." Metaphorically, a mountain is a "breast" that rises up from the plain; and certainly a mountain is a symbol of strength. If we combine these several ideas, we might say that "El Shaddai" is the name of "the all-powerful and all-sufficient God who can do anything and meet any need."

But why would God reveal this name to Abraham at this time, at the close of thirteen years of silence? Because God was going to tell His friend that Sarah would have a son. The Lord wanted Abraham to know that He is the God who is all-sufficient and all-powerful, and that nothing is too hard for Him. God says "I will" twelve times in this chapter; He is about to do the miraculous.

After Abraham's battle with the four kings, God came to him as a warrior and told him He was his "shield." When Abraham wondered about his refusal of Sodom's wealth, God told him He was his "exceedingly great reward" (Gen. 15:1). Now when Abraham and Sarah were "as good as dead," God assured them that He was more than sufficient to bring about the miracle birth. God comes to us in the ways we need Him most. — *Old Testament - The Bible Exposition Commentary – Pentateuch.*

6. Verse 1. Abraham is called to be blameless. What does it mean to be blameless? Does it mean perfect?

Abram is also commanded to be "blameless" (תָּמִים, tāmîm), a word that does not imply moral perfection but "wholeness" or "soundness." It is often used of sacrificial animals which are healthy and without injury or visible blemish. — *The College Press NIV Commentary – Genesis, Volume 2.*

7. Should we seek to be perfect?

Revelation always brings responsibility. Enoch and Noah had walked with God (5:22; 6:8-9), but Abraham was to walk before God, that is, live in the knowledge that the eyes of God were always upon him (Heb. 4:13). The word "perfect" does not mean "sinless," for that would be an impossible goal for anyone to reach (1 Kings 8:46). The word means "single-hearted, without blame, sincere, wholly devoted to the Lord." In Exodus 12:5, the word refers to a "perfect" sacrifice without blemish. It was a call for integrity.

This is not to suggest that God's people should settle for anything less than striving to conform to His will. "His desire for us should be our aim and desire for ourselves," wrote Alexander Maclaren. "It is more blessed to be smitten with the longing to win the unwon than to stagnate in ignoble contentment with partial attainments. Better to climb, with faces turned upwards to the inaccessible peak, than to lie at ease in the fat valleys" (Expositions of Holy Scripture, vol. 1, 120 [Baker Book House, 1974]).

The secret of a perfect walk before God is a personal worship of God. Like Abraham, every believer must fall before the Lord and yield everything to Him. If He is "El Shaddai—God Almighty," then who are we to resist His will? — *Old Testament - The Bible Exposition Commentary – Pentateuch.*

8. We never will be perfect. Why try?

The Apostle John said, "My dear children, I write this to you so that you will not sin" (1 John 2:1). The whole purpose of John's letter, he says, is that we not sin. One day as I was studying this chapter I realized that my personal life's objective regarding holiness was less than that of John's. He was saying, in effect, "Make it your aim not to sin." As I thought about this, I realized that deep within my heart my real aim was not to sin very much. I found it difficult to say, "Yes, Lord, from here on I will make it my aim not to sin." I realized God was calling me that day to a deeper level of commitment to holiness than I had previously been willing to make.

Can you imagine a soldier going into battle with the aim of "not getting hit very much"? The very suggestion is ridiculous. His aim is not to get hit at all! Yet if we have not made a commitment to holiness without exception, we are like a soldier going into battle with the aim of not getting hit very much. We can be sure if that is our aim, we will be hit—not with bullets, but with temptation over and over again. — Jerry Bridges, *The Pursuit of Holiness* (Colorado Springs: Navpress, 1978), 92–93.

9. God called Abraham to walk before Him. What does it mean to walk with God? How do we walk with God?

"Walk before Me," the Lord told Abram (Genesis 17:1, NASB). The Lord could have chosen any number of verbs of motion: crawl, move, run. He could have said, "Hurry along—make up for lost time." He chose instead the image of placing one foot in front of the other, repetitively and consistently. Walking is an action that carries someone from one place to another— remember, the story of Abram uses a journey motif—and (this is important) it's a sustainable action over the long haul. Sprints cover short distances and leave you exhausted. A marathon demands everything you have to run the race and then requires days of recuperation afterward. But the average person can walk for miles each day and actually gain strength. (In fact, my doctor strongly recommends it!)

Take note of the unusual preposition in God's command. Usually we think of someone walking with another. The Hebrew preposition before conveys "for, in regard to." We understand that the walking isn't literal; it's an analogy referring to Abram's relationship with God. "Walk in regard to Me, doing the right things repetitively and consistently, day after day, over the long run of your life. Do this as I call the cadence."

Anyone who has served in the military knows the term cadence all too well. My first days in a Marine Corps boot camp began before sunrise with strength training and marching. In the Marines, the "almighty" is your drill instructor! The place where you learn to march is called "the grinder," an expansive asphalt surface dedicated to the instruction of marching and close-order drill. For hours, recruits learn the voice of their master and practice walking in step. A single voice keeps dozens of individuals in a company walking together in the same direction. Without the cadence, there is chaos.

The grinder usually has more than one company of recruits marching at the same time. Each company must learn to hear the unique voice of their drill instructor. And trust me—it doesn't take long before you're attuned to that inimitable bark of your drill instructor. In only a few weeks, you're able to detect his voice in any crowd at any time.

In a sense, El-Shaddai commanded Abram, "Walk with Me as I call the cadence." — Charles R. Swindoll, *Abraham: One Nomad's Amazing Journey of Faith* (Carol Stream, IL: Tyndale, 2014).

10. Was God asking Abraham to change?

While the Lord urged Abram to walk with Him and to be blameless, it should be clear that God wasn't asking him to do anything new or different. I believe that over the past thirteen years, it had become Abram's habit to walk with God, becoming increasingly "complete, whole, sound, unimpaired." The Lord affirmed his faithful walk and encouraged him to continue. In the sustained years of silence, Abram became a man of deep faith.

In his book Celebration of Discipline, Richard Foster writes, "Superficiality is the curse of our age. The doctrine of instant satisfaction is a primary spiritual problem. The desperate need today is not for a greater number of intelligent people, or gifted people, but for deep people."[23] I challenge you to be on the lookout for deep people. Look carefully. You won't find an overabundance. Our schools turn out lots of educated people. Top companies find the most intelligent people. Gifted people flock to New York, Hollywood, Las Vegas, and Nashville. But people of depth are rare. Not many people have the foresight or the patience to cultivate spiritually deep roots. — Charles R. Swindoll, *Abraham: One Nomad's Amazing Journey of Faith* (Carol Stream, IL: Tyndale, 2014).

11. Abraham fell facedown before the Lord. When you pray, do you ever fall facedown? What does it mean to fall facedown? Why did Abraham fall facedown?

The Scriptures declare, "Abram fell on his face" as the Lord talked with him (Genesis 17:3). Abraham was reverent and submissive. Probably there is no better picture anywhere in the Bible of the right place for mankind and the right place for God. God was on His throne speaking, and Abraham was on his face listening!

Where God and man are in relationship, this must be the ideal. God must be the communicator, and man must be in the listening, obeying attitude. If men and women are not willing to assume this listening attitude, there will be no meeting with God in living, personal experience....

Yes, Abraham was lying facedown in humility and reverence, overcome with awe in this encounter with God. He knew that he was surrounded by the world's greatest mystery. The presence of this One who fills all things was pressing in upon him, rising above him, defeating him, taking away his natural self-confidence. God was overwhelming him and yet inviting and calling him, pleading with him and promising him a great future as a friend of God! — A. W. Tozer, *Tozer on Christian Leadership: A 366-Day Devotional* (Camp Hill, PA: WingSpread, 2001).

12. What does praying facedown do for us that praying in a chair does not?

Those who heard Luther's prayers have told us of the tremendous effect they often had upon the listeners. He would begin in moving humility, his spirit facedown in utter self-abnegation, and sometimes rise to a boldness of petition that would startle the hearers.

There is among us today a pseudo-mysticism which affects a tender intimacy with God but lacks that breathless awe which the true worshiper must always feel in the presence of the Holy God. This simpering spirit sometimes expresses itself in religious baby talk wholly unworthy of those who are addressing the Most High.

To hear a so-called Christian ... addressing words of saccharine sweetness to one whom he or she calls "Jesus dear," is a shocking experience for anyone who has once seen heaven opened and stood speechless before the Holy Presence. No one who has ever bowed before the Burning Bush can thereafter speak lightly of God, much less be guilty of levity in addressing Him.

When Horace Bushnell prayed in the field under the night sky, his friend who knelt by his side drew in his arms close to his body. "I was afraid to stretch out my hands," he said, "lest I touch God." — *Tozer on the Almighty God : A 366-Day Devotional* (Camp Hill, PA: WingSpread, 2004).

13. Verse 4. What is the significance of this name change?

The name change from Abram ("exalted father") to Abraham ("father of many") indicates the sovereign authority of El-Shaddai and an additional pledge that God would fulfill his promise. Every time Abraham and Sarah heard their new names, they would be reminded of God's promise and encouraged by his faithfulness. In these verses Abraham was quiet before God, who did all the talking.

Five promises appear in the passage, beginning with I will make you very fruitful. How interesting that one of the blessings God gave to Abraham was the joy of children, the joy of fathering Ishmael and Isaac, initially in his own family and then through other descendants as the nation grew. The second promise, I will make nations of you, expanded the first. The word nations appears in the plural. We think of Abraham as the father of the Jewish nation, but he was also the father of all Arabs. This promise that God would make Abraham into great nations reminds us of chapter 12 where the initial promise was given (12:1-3). — *Holman Old Testament Commentary – Genesis*.

14. Verse 8. When did Israel fully possess the land promised to Abraham?

Joshua led them into their land where they conquered the inhabitants and claimed their inheritance. But the people did not stay true to the covenant, so God had to discipline them in the land (Judges 2:10-23). He raised up enemy nations to defeat Israel and put her in bondage. Israel was in the land, but she did not control it or enjoy it (Deut. 28:15ff).

During the reigns of David and Solomon, the people enjoyed their inheritance and served the Lord faithfully. But after the kingdom divided, Israel and Judah both decayed spiritually (except for occasional interludes of revival) and ended up in bondage: Assyria defeated Israel, and Babylon conquered Judah. It was then that God disciplined His people outside their land. It was as though He were saying, "You have polluted My land with your idols, so I will put you in a land that is addicted to idols. Get your fill of it! After you have been away from your land for seventy years, maybe you will learn to appreciate what I gave you."

God permitted a remnant to return to the land, rebuild the city and the temple, and restore the nation; but it never became a great power again. However, whether Israel is faithful or faithless, the land belongs to her; and one day she will inherit it and enjoy it to the glory of God. Israel's title deed to the land is a vital part of God's everlasting covenant with Abraham. — *Old Testament - The Bible Exposition Commentary – Pentateuch.*

15. Verse 9. What was required of Abraham in this covenant?

17:9-14. In verse 9 we learn that this covenant, everlasting though it may be from God's perspective, required a response from Abraham and his descendants. God also provided a symbol of this human response: You are to undergo circumcision. This was not some new physical sign that God created just for this occasion. In fact, circumcision was well-known in ancient times and was practiced by many of the nations among which Abraham lived. — *Holman Old Testament Commentary – Genesis.*

16. What was God's part of the covenant?

The Lord then revealed more details concerning His plan to redeem the world through the nation of Israel. His predictions took the form of several unconditional promises. Five times, the Lord affirmed, "I will . . ." (see Genesis 17:5-8, ESV).

- "I will make you exceedingly fruitful."

- "I will make you into nations, and kings shall come from you."

- "I will establish my covenant between me and you and your offspring."

- "I will give to you and to your offspring after you the land of your sojournings, all the land of Canaan."

- "I will be their God."

In this way, God essentially said, "These are the things you can count on. I will do them. They are My responsibility. And Abraham, remember that El-Shaddai is speaking to you. I will see to it that these things take place. Never doubt it, even when you're not hearing from Me or when life appears stagnant. I will never forget to fulfill what I promised." — Charles R. Swindoll, *Abraham: One Nomad's Amazing Journey of Faith* (Carol Stream, IL: Tyndale, 2014).

17. Why do you suppose God waited so long to give Abraham and Sarah a son? What was He trying to do to them? What is the lesson for us?

In being fruitful for God, we have nothing in ourselves that will accomplish the task. Abraham and Sarah had tried their own plan, and it failed miserably. Jesus said, "Without Me, ye can do nothing" (John 15:5). "We say that we depend on the Holy Spirit," wrote Vance Havner, "but actually we are so wired up with our own devices that if the fire does not fall from heaven, we can turn on a switch and produce false fire of our own."

I read about a young Scottish minister who walked proudly into the pulpit to preach his first sermon. He had a brilliant mind and a good education and was confident of himself as he faced his first congregation. But the longer he preached, the more conscious everyone was that "the Lord was not in the wind." He finished his message quickly and came down from the pulpit with his head bowed, his pride now gone. Afterward, one of the members said to him, "If you had gone into the pulpit the way you came down, you might have come down from the pulpit the way you went up." — *Old Testament - The Bible Exposition Commentary – Pentateuch.*

18. Has it ever felt like God was silent for a long time in your life? Who has a story? Why is God sometimes silent?

God had not spoken directly to Abraham for thirteen years, ever since he had taken matters into his own hands to produce a godly seed. Abraham was already eighty-six years old when Hagar bore him Ishmael (Gen. 16:16), and he was ninety-nine years old when the Lord appeared to him again (17:1).

The Silence of Winter

"It must have been a terrible ordeal," states F. B. Meyer, "driving him back on the promise which had been given and searching his heart to ascertain if the cause lay within himself. Such silences have always exercised the hearts of God's saints, leading them to say with the Psalmist: 'Be not silent to me: lest, if thou be silent to me, I become like them that go down into the pit' (Ps. 28:1). And yet they are to the heart what the silence of winter is to the world of nature, in preparing it for the outburst of spring." — Gene A. Getz, *Men of Character: Abraham* (Nashville: B&H, 1996).

19. Verse 17. How do you interpret Abraham's laughter here?

This does seem like strange behavior since Abraham's mistake was no laughing matter. Why would he question God's power to give Sarah and him a son in their old age, especially in view of God's reassuring words (17:16)? More importantly, why would he cry out to God: "If only Ishmael might live under your blessing!" (17:18)?

Some believe that this must have been an exclamation of joy. But how could it be? I believe this was a nervous laugh. It was a laugh reflecting doubt and confusion—and embarrassment.

Abraham's reactions were those of a man who for thirteen years felt he was right and suddenly discovered he was wrong. He was a man who had placed his total hope in Ishmael as the promised seed. He had come to love this boy in spite of his wild nature (16:12). It was only logical for him to defend himself and his son at this moment, to question God about the event and to plead for Ishmael. — Gene A. Getz, *Men of Character: Abraham* (Nashville: B&H, 1996).

20. How did God respond to Abraham? What is the lesson for us?

God's response to Abraham was both positive and negative. God would bless Ishmael as He had promised (17:20). "But," God said, "my covenant I will establish with Isaac, whom Sarah will bear to you by this time next year" (17:21). It's no wonder Abraham was shocked, nervous, and nonplused. These promises sounded so similar.

Although Abraham's thought patterns all these years seemed logical and rational, they were built on a false premise that led to false conclusions. Like any one of us, Abraham had difficulty accepting the fact that he had made such a serious mistake. How would you feel if you suddenly discovered that you had been outside of the will of God when for thirteen years you thought you were in the will of God? It would be a shattering blow to any man's ego. Frankly, I'd be on my face laughing, too, not for joy, but from embarrassment.

For the first time in more than a decade, Abraham was able to understand God's revelation to him (15:5) as well as the message God had spoken to Hagar (16:10). Gradually, everything came into focus. God had in mind two sons. The first was Isaac, and the second was Ishmael. The first blessing was for the true heir. The second blessing was for the son who was born according to the flesh. Centuries later, Paul referred to these two boys when he said of Abraham: "His son by the slave woman was born in the ordinary way; but his son by the free woman was born as the result of a promise" (Gal. 4:23). — Gene A. Getz, *Men of Character: Abraham* (Nashville: B&H, 1996).

21. Summarize this story. What is the lesson for us?

The most encouraging part of this story is its ending. Abraham, true man of God that he was, took immediate steps to get back on the right track. He acknowledged his error. Although he had to live with the results of his mistake, he immediately began to obey God's Word.

The Lord gave Abraham a new contract, a covenant in the flesh. He and all the males in his family were to be circumcised, which would be a sign of separation from all that is contrary to the will of God. Eager to obey God, Abraham followed through immediately. — Gene A. Getz, *Men of Character: Abraham* (Nashville: B&H, 1996).

22. How can we support one another in prayer this week?

Prayer is not a convenient device for imposing our will upon God, or bending his will to ours, but the prescribed way of subordinating our will to his. —John Stott

Prayer is the spiritual gymnasium in which we exercise and practice godliness. —V. L. Crawford

The great tragedy of life is not unanswered prayer, but unoffered prayer. —F. B. Meyer

Campus Life's Ignite Your Faith, *Ignite Your Faith: 365 Devotions to Set Your Faith on Fire* (Grand Rapids, MI: Revell, 2009).

Genesis, Lesson #10
Good Questions Have Small Groups Talking
www.joshhunt.com

Genesis 18.20 – 25; 19.12 - 16

OPEN

Let's each your name and one thing you are grateful for this week.

DIG

1. **Let's look at this story as a whole from a couple of different perspectives. What does this story teach us about God?**

   Henry M. Morris applies the chapter like this: "The modern world, America in particular, has had the witness of the Christian gospel for a long time. But mankind has rejected it, and is descending into a morass of corruption and wickedness even greater than that of the pagan world before Christ. He has assured mankind, through his Word, that they will soon be coming to judgment. Until then, his people have the responsibility of intercessory prayer for lost men, and of a consistent spiritual witness to them, warning them of the wrath to come. In particular, as was true of Abraham, it is especially true that believers command their children to keep the way of the Lord."

   In Genesis 18 and 19 we find (1) the certainty of divine judgment, (2) an example of prayerful intercession for others, (3) mercy on the part of God, and (4) halfhearted and nearly ineffective obedience by a believer and his family. — *Boice*

Expositional Commentary - An Expositional Commentary – Genesis, Volume 2: A New Beginning (Genesis 12-36).

2. Would you like God better if chapters like this were not in the Bible?

Nothing is so offensive to the unregenerate mind as a message of coming judgment for sin. But the chief reason is precisely that the people involved are sinners. If God had told Abraham that he was about to destroy him, Abraham would have been puzzled in view of God's earlier promises, but he would not have claimed injustice on the part of God. Abraham knew he had no claim on God and that anything he had ever received from God was due to God's mercy. Abraham would have said with Job, "Naked I came from my mother's womb, and naked I will depart. The Lord gave and the Lord has taken away; may the name of the Lord be praised" (Job 1:21). He would have said with Paul, "Let God be true, and every man a liar" (Rom. 3:4). — *Boice Expositional Commentary - An Expositional Commentary – Genesis, Volume 2: A New Beginning (Genesis 12-36).*

3. Can people grow so wicked, so pagan, so vile that God justifiably destroys them? Can leaders be so evil and cruel that God, knowing the hardness of their hearts, righteously removes them from the earth?

Apparently so. He did so with Sodom and Gomorrah (Gen. 19:24–25). He did so with the Hittites, Amorites, Canaanites, Hivites, and Jebusites (Ex. 23:23).

In those towns that the LORD your God is giving you as a special possession, destroy every living thing . . . This will prevent the people of the land from teaching you to imitate their detestable customs in the worship of their gods, which would cause you to sin deeply against the LORD your God. (Deut. 20:16, 18 NLT)

God has used warfare as a form of judgment against the enemies of God. In fact, he uses warfare as judgment against his own people when they become enemies of God.

God's priority is the salvation of souls. When a people group blockades his plan, does he not have the right to remove them? He is the God who knows "the end from the beginning" (Isa. 46:10). He knows the hearts of everyone and protects his people by punishing the evil of their wicked neighbors. Is it not God's right to punish evil? Is it not appropriate for the One who tells us to hate that which is evil to punish that which is evil? Of course it is.

I like the words of C. S. Lewis here:

> Does loving your enemy mean not punishing him? No, for loving myself does not mean that I ought not to subject myself to punishment—even to death. If one had committed a murder, the right Christian thing to do would be to give yourself up to the police and be hanged. It is, therefore, in my opinion, perfectly right for a Christian judge to sentence a man to death or a Christian soldier to kill an enemy. I always have thought so, ever since I became a Christian and long before the war, and I still think so now that we are at peace. It is no good quoting "Thou shalt not kill." There are two Greek words: the ordinary word to kill and the word to murder. And when Christ quotes that commandment He uses the murder one in all three accounts, Matthew, Mark, and Luke. And I am told there is the same distinction in Hebrew. All killing is not murder any more than all sexual intercourse is adultery. When soldiers came to St. John the Baptist asking what to do, he never remotely suggested that they ought to leave the army: nor did Christ when He met a Roman sergeant-major—what they called a centurion. The idea of the knight—the Christian in arms for the defence of a good cause—is one of the great Christian ideas. War is a dreadful thing, and I can respect an honest pacifist, though I think he is entirely mistaken. — Max Lucado, *Max on Life: Answers and Inspiration for Today's Questions* (Nashville: Thomas Nelson, 2011).

4. What does this story teach us about prayer?

It was studying Genesis 18 that taught saintly George Mueller of Bristol, that modern giant of faith, one of the most important secrets of prayer. It taught him to use argument in pleading his case before God. He would remind the Lord that the orphan boys and girls entrusted to his care were not his orphans, they were God's. Had he not declared Himself to be the Father of the fatherless? It was God's work, not Mueller's. He was but the instrument. If it were God's work, was not God bound to take care of it? Could God suffer His glory to be diminished? Was not a half-believing church looking on and a wholly unbelieving world? Must not God silence the jibing tongue? Must He not silence the scoffer and the skeptic? Thus George Mueller prayed and thus he received truly astonishing answers from God. And thus Abraham prayed, besieging his heavenly visitor with plea after plea. — *The John Phillips Commentary Series – Exploring Genesis: An Expository Commentary.*

5. Has anyone been shopping in the Orient? What light does shopping in the Orient shed on this story?

Like a true oriental, Abraham actually bargained with God. Anyone who has been in an eastern market knows how it goes: "How much do you want for this silk scarf?"

"Fifty piasters."

"Fifty piasters! Ill give you five."

At that point the merchant seems about to break a blood vessel. He calls all his ancestors to witness the insult that has been heaped upon him. Finally he says, "Forty-five."

"Nonsense," says the buyer, "I can get one next door without being robbed." He returns the scarf to the seller. But mention of the competition evokes a further reduction in price. "As Allah is my witness I'll be ruined. Thirty piasters!" And the merchant throws down the scarf in disgust.

The purchaser walks out of the shop and heads next door, but before a dozen steps can be taken the shopkeeper comes hurrying out too, wringing his hands and calling on his god. "Come back! Come back! You can have it for twenty."

The purchaser returns to the shop, picks up the merchandise and looks at it with critical disdain. The merchant is ready. He picks a gaudy silk handkerchief. "Twenty piasters—and I'll throw in this matchless handkerchief of finest Damascus silk. May Allah witness I am being ruined; what can I do? I have a large family. Twenty piasters and this silk handkerchief free."

The purchaser takes out his wallet and places ten piasters on the counter. He picks up the scarf. "Ten piasters, Abdullah, and that's my final offer. Ten piasters and you can keep your handkerchief."

That is how it went between Abraham and God. He bargained with God as he would bargain in the suk. He haggled, as it were, over the price. What would God take? How many souls would be needed to save Sodom? It was done with great daring but also with very great dignity and awe. "Lord, suppose there are fifty righteous? Suppose it lacks five of the fifty? What about forty-five? Forty? Twenty? Ten?" And each time the living God, with infinite condescension, came down until at last Abraham stopped at ten. — *The John Phillips Commentary Series – Exploring Genesis: An Expository Commentary.*

6. Would you feel comfortable negotiating with God this way? Should we feel comfortable negotiating with God this way?

Abraham kept the negotiating session going. If the Lord had responded to the number of 50, would He respond to 45? He would. And so it went, from 40 to 30 to 20…and finally to 10—as far as the patriarch dared to go.

It might almost seem irreverent the way Abraham "dickered" with the Lord in this conversation. In reality, however, it reveals the closeness of their friendship. It's also a reflection of the way business was done in the Middle East. You always bargained for a deal, never paying the original asking price.

Abraham was doing business with the Lord, and the most significant point about this conversation was that he already knew he had the heart of the Lord in this prayer. He could pray and plead with God in confidence, knowing that He was just and merciful, a God who truly didn't want to bring calamity on people. — Greg Laurie, *The Greatest Stories Ever Told, Volume One* (Dana Point, CA: Kerygma Publishing—Allen David Books, 2011).

7. Why do you suppose Abraham stopped his negotiation at 10? Why not 5 or less?

He stopped at ten. Up until then he had complete assurance that God would hear and respond, but at the figure ten all such assurance stopped. He had arrived at the divinely set limit, and so well attuned was Abraham to the mind and will of God that he instinctively knew that he must go no lower than ten.

But why was ten the number? Suppose Abraham had gone on to five. He could still not have saved Sodom, for there were not five righteous souls in that place. There were only four who responded in the crucial hour. There were five cities in the plain. In Scripture two is the number of adequate witness, so it required ten righteous people to be in the valley, else there would not be even the minimum witness for God. Then, too, Abraham probably believed that there would be ten righteous souls in Sodom. There were Lot and his wife and his two unmarried daughters who lived in his house—that made four. There were his sons-in-law (the text uses the plural, not the dual, implying that there would be at least three of them) who, together with their wives, would make another six, thus making ten in all. So for one reason or another Abraham lost all liberty to pray further when he arrived at the number ten. — *The John Phillips Commentary Series – Exploring Genesis: An Expository Commentary.*

8. **Why didn't God grant Abraham's request? Why does He sometimes say "No" to our prayers?**

   Abraham went to the Lord with his petition to save Sodom and Gomorrah. God heard his request, and although He did not grant it the way Abraham had hoped, the conversation that took place between them deepened their relationship.

   God wants to grant our requests, but we make it impossible for Him to do so when we ask for things that contradict His righteous, loving character. What would you do if your child asked for something that would cause him or her harm? Love for your child would demand that you deny the request.

   We need to continually seek Him to ensure that our petitions and our motives are in line with His will. Then, whether He says yes, no, or wait, our prayers will draw us ever closer to Him. — Charles R. Swindoll, *Faith for the Journey: Daily Meditations on Courageous Trust in* God (Carol Stream, IL: Tyndale, 2014).

9. **Let me remind you of a high-dollar word: anthropomorphic. In verse 20 we have an example of anthropomorphic language. See if you can find it?**

   The language is anthropomorphic to be sure, for divine omniscience knew all about the sins of Sodom and Gomorrah. But this close scrutiny of God was a way of communicating his careful justice; he would not destroy the people of the plain unless he was absolutely sure they were wicked enough for severe punishment. — Allen Ross and John N. Oswalt, *Cornerstone Biblical Commentary: Genesis, Exodus, vol. 1* (Carol Stream, IL: Tyndale House Publishers, 2008), 126.

10. **Anthropomorphic language is quite common in Scripture. Can you think of examples?**

    OT (some examples)

    A. Physical body parts

1. eyes—Gen. 1:4, 31; 6:8; Exod. 33:17; Num. 14:14; Deut. 11:12; Zech. 4:10

2. hands—Exod. 15:17; Num. 11:23; Deut. 2:15

3. arm—Exod. 6:6; 15:16; Num. 11:23; Deut. 4:34; 5:15

4. ears—Num. 11:18; 1 Sam. 8:21; 2 Kgs. 19:16; Ps. 5:1; 10:17; 18:6

5. face—Exod. 32:30; 33:11; Num. 6:25; Deut. 34:10; Ps. 114:7

6. finger—Exod. 8:19; 31:18; Deut. 9:10; Ps. 8:3

7. voice—Gen. 3:8, 10; Exod. 15:26; 19:19; Deut. 26:17; 27:10

8. feet—Exod. 24:10; Ezek. 43:7

9. human form—Exod. 24:9–11; Ps. 47; Isa. 6:1; Ezek. 1:26

10. the angel of the Lord—Gen. 16:7–13; 22:11–15; 31:11, 13; 48:15–16; Exod. 3:4, 13–21; 14:19; Jdgs. 2:1; 6:22–23; 13:3–22

B. Physical actions

1. speaking as the mechanism of creation—Gen. 1:3, 6, 9, 11, 14, 20, 24, 26

2. walking (i.e., sound of) in Eden—Gen. 3:8; 18:33; Hab. 3:15

3. closing the door of Noah's ark—Gen. 7:16

4. smelling sacrifices—Gen. 8:21; Lev. 26:31; Amos 5:21

5. coming down—Gen. 11:5; 18:21; Exod. 3:8; 19:11, 18, 20

6. burying Moses—Deut. 34:6

Bob Utley, *Ezekiel, Study Guide Commentary Series* (Marshall, TX: Bible Lessons International, 2008), 8.

11. Why does the Bible use anthropomorphic language so often?

Of course, God doesn't literally have internal dialogues with Himself the way we do. Presenting the Almighty in this human manner is another literary technique called anthropomorphism. It portrays God, an infinite and indescribable Being, in human terms that help us understand Him better. In this case, the narrator allows us to see God's motivation for including Abraham in His plans to address the evil of Sodom and Gomorrah. The Lord said, in effect, "I have chosen Abraham and his descendants to be My human representatives before all the other people of the world. To equip him for the job, I need to give him insider's knowledge on what I'm doing and why. The way I deal with Sodom and Gomorrah will be his first official lesson as My human assistant."

Based on His decision to include Abraham in His plans, the Lord engaged the patriarch in a dialogue. God knew from the beginning what He would do. He's omniscient; He knows future events before they occur. — Charles R. Swindoll, *Abraham: One Nomad's Amazing Journey of Faith* (Carol Stream, IL: Tyndale, 2014).

12. Genesis 19.15 mentions angels. What does the Bible teach about angels? What do angels do?

And when they get here, angels have a special work to accomplish in the lives of believers. Hebrews 1:14 tells us that angels are "ministering spirits sent out to serve for the sake of those who are to inherit salvation." We witness angels rescuing Lot and his family from the destruction of Sodom (see Gen. 19:16), for example.

In Billy Graham's classic book Angels: God's Secret Agents, we learn about John G. Paton, a nineteenth-century missionary to the New Hebrides Islands, where cannibals held sway. On one particular night, Paton and his wife were in their home at the mission station and got word of an imminent attack by an indigenous group. Knowing this, John and his wife began to pray. Hours passed, however, and all was peaceful; no attack ever came. The next morning, there was no sign of their enemies, and the missionary couple wondered what had happened.

A year or so later, the chief of the tribe that had wanted to kill the Patons received Jesus Christ as his Savior. One day, John said to him, "I have to ask you what happened that night when you were coming to kill us. Why didn't you follow through on it?" The chief replied, "What do you mean, why didn't we go through with it? Who were all of those men there with you?"

"There were no men there," Paton replied.

But the chief would have none of it. "We didn't attack," he said, "because there were hundreds of big men in shining garments with drawn swords, circling the mission station."

And in that moment, John knew that he and his wife had been guarded by a contingent of angels. — Greg Laurie, *As It Is in Heaven: How Eternity Brings Focus to What Really Matters* (Carol Stream, IL: Tyndale, 2014).

13. What is an angel?

An angel is a living being who has a personality (intellect, emotion, and will). Angels do not have physical bodies, but can manifest themselves physically. Angels are powerful, but they are not omnipotent; wise, but not omniscient. There are great numbers of them, but they are not limitless. An angel's main task is to minister to God or for God (Heb. 1:13). — Elmer Towns, *Bible Answers for Almost All Your Questions* (Nashville: Thomas Nelson, 2003).

14. How smart are angels?

Angels are exceedingly wise and knowledgeable, but not omniscient, meaning they do not know all things at all times. Only God knows all things at all times. The knowledge of angels is limited, as Jesus said, "But of that day and hour no one knows, not even the angels of heaven, but My Father only" (Matt. 24:36). However, angels can learn new things. Notice what Peter said: "Things which angels desire to look into" (1 Pet. 1:12). The angels do not understand all of the ramifications of the gospel, but according to Peter they are learning from us. — Elmer Towns, *Bible Answers for Almost All Your Questions* (Nashville: Thomas Nelson, 2003).

15. Can angels sin?

When Lucifer fell, apparently a group of angels fell with him. Many teach that one-third of all the angels fell with Lucifer (Rev. 12:4). Those angels which have fallen into sin are "confirmed in wickedness," meaning they cannot be converted, nor can they do good. Those angels that chose to follow God are "confirmed in holiness," which means they can only do good and cannot be lost in hell.

Some people feel it is wrong to say angels do not have another chance of sinning. However, that will be the condition of every Christian once he dies; when we get to heaven we will lose our sin nature, not being able to sin. — Elmer Towns, *Bible Answers for Almost All Your Questions* (Nashville: Thomas Nelson, 2003).

16. What do angels do for us today?

Angels apparently deliver us at our deaths into the presence of God. Lazarus "was carried by the angels to Abraham's bosom" (Luke 16:22). Angels also deliver messages for God (Rev. 22:8, Luke 1:26–27). — Elmer Towns, *Bible Answers for Almost All Your Questions* (Nashville: Thomas Nelson, 2003).

17. Can angels read our minds?

No. Only God knows the thoughts of all people, because only God knows all things at all times. However, angels can understand our external actions; therefore, they have some understanding of what is going on in our minds. — Elmer Towns, *Bible Answers for Almost All Your Questions* (Nashville: Thomas Nelson, 2003).

18. What do our guardian angels do for us?

Children are described as having "their angels" (Matt. 18:10). When Rhoda was guarding the door while Peter knocked for entrance, the person at the door was described as "his angel" (Acts 12:15). Apparently, some thought Peter might have died and his angel appeared at the house.

God protects His people by angels. The Bible says, "The angel of the LORD encamps all around those who fear Him, and delivers them" (Ps. 34:7) Guardian angels "always see the face of [Jesus'] Father who is in heaven" (Matt. 18:10), implying that God knows when we are in danger, and sends a guardian angel to help us. Origen, one of the early church fathers, said, "We must say that every human soul is under direction of an angel who is like a father." St. Basil said, "An angel is put in charge of every believer, providing we do not drive them out by sin. He guards the soul like an army." The angel protects the physical aspect of our lives, whereas the Holy Spirit protects the spiritual aspect of our lives. — Elmer Towns, *Bible Answers for Almost All Your Questions* (Nashville: Thomas Nelson, 2003).

19. Genesis 19.16. Why did Lot hesitate? What is the lesson for us?

TO THE OBJECTIVE observer, Lot and his wife were downright foolish. They had built their home on an island in a cesspool, and when death loomed overhead, they didn't want to leave. We might struggle to see these historical figures as real people just like us, and if we're not careful, we will judge Lot and his wife too harshly. The fact is, in many ways, we're no different. Though we're separated by 3,500 years, several thousand miles, and a language, we struggle with the same frailties and desires of human nature.

So why could Lot —regarded in the New Testament as a righteous man (see 2 Peter 2:8) —live comfortably in Sodom? It was because his perception of reality had gradually become distorted. He made sense of his senseless choices with small excuses and minor rationalizations.

Perhaps you're not as deluded as Lot and his wife. Still, reflect on your current situation. Try to see your life objectively. What are you putting up with? Where are you compromising? It may be that you're allowing pornography to pollute your home or your mind. It may be that you're keeping the secrets of an abusive partner, who causes you or others continual harm. It may be that you're fudging financial records where you work, which you have rationalized in your mind because this helps you provide for your family.

Don't be fooled. If it's wrong, it's a big deal. If it's a habitual wrong, it's a bigger deal. It's time for all of us to open our eyes and examine our homes, our neighborhoods, and our nations objectively. We must not compromise on what God has revealed to us is right and good. — Charles R. Swindoll, *Faith for the Journey: Daily Meditations on Courageous Trust in God* (Carol Stream, IL: Tyndale, 2014).

20. When Lot hesitated, the angel took him by the hand and hurried him along. What do we learn about God from this?

BIBLE COMMENTATORS AREN'T SURE WHY Lot lingered after the angels told him to flee Sodom because they were going to destroy it. Some believe he was hesitant because of the property he would lose. Some believe he was waiting to see if his two sons-in-law would leave the city (v. 14). And some believe he grieved for everyone inside. Maybe it was a combination of all three.

In spite of his lingering, the angels showed mercy to Lot, his wife, and their two adult daughters, grabbing them by the hand and leading them out of the city. Lot was undeserving of this mercy. In fact, our modern culture would probably say, "Lot was no angel," given that he offered his two daughters to a mob, and then, once safely tucked away in a cave with his daughters, he got drunk and fell prey to their advances.

But redemption isn't about acting like an angel; instead, it's a power that transforms people who once had no regard for their sin into redeemed sinners who spend their entire lives putting the old sin nature to death. And even though the journey is difficult, they do so with an everlasting joy.

We don't know if Lot did this, but we're certainly called to live that way. — Compiled By Barbour Staff, *The Men of the Bible Devotional: Insights from the Warriors, Wimps, and Wise Guys* (Uhrichsville, OH: Barbour, 2015).

21. Review / Overview. How was it that Lot and family was saved from this destruction? What is the lesson for us?

Abraham standing alone with God is the key to the rescue of Lot and his family, out they come whether they like it or not. The angels are insistent in answer to Abraham's intercession (see v. 16). Yet Lot was rescued with the greatest difficulty because of his vacillation. Vacillation in a crisis is the sign of an unabandoned nature. An abandoned nature never can vacillate because there is nothing to weigh; such a nature is completely abandoned to another. Lot's fear was culpable because it was indicative of a stultified judgment.

See to it that you do not profane the holiness of God by refusing to abandon yourself away from your experience of what He has done for you to God Himself. Whenever you do not come in contact with God for yourself, you will begin to watch your own whiteness—I dare not say this or do that. It is a cabined, confined life and when difficulties come like a wall of fire, God has to come and rescue you; and He does it by means of intercession on the part of some one else. Beware of accepting the blessings and visions of God as an indication of your goodness and not of the mercy and purpose of God— "the Lord being merciful unto him." — Oswald Chambers, *Not Knowing Where (*Grand Rapids: Discovery House, 1996).

22. Let's wrap up with the same question we began with—what does the story of Sodom and Gomorrah teach us about God?

One of his more unusual sermons was preached some time later in a village near Evans Mills, New York. During the service, Finney, who seldom prepared his sermons in advance, asked God to give him a text. Suddenly he remembered the story of Sodom, city of Lot. Genesis 19:14 rushed to mind : "Get up, get out of this place; for the Lord will destroy this city!"

In his sermon, Finney painted the condition of Sodom before God destroyed it. I had not spoken in this strain more than a quarter hour when an awful solemnity seemed to settle upon them; the congregation began to fall from their seats in every direction and cried for mercy. If I had had a sword in each hand, I could not have cut them down as fast as they fell. Everyone prayed who was able to speak at all.

Only afterward Finney learned the village where he preached was known as Sodom, and the man who had invited him was called Lot. — Robert J. Morgan, *From This Verse: 365 Scriptures That Changed the World, electronic ed.* (Nashville: Thomas Nelson Publishers, 2000).

Genesis, Lesson #11
Good Questions Have Small Groups Talking
www.joshhunt.com

Genesis 21.1 - 8

OPEN

Let's each your name and what show do you tend to turn to when you want a good laugh?

DIG

1. **Let's look at this story as a whole. What is the application to our lives?**

   Do you have trouble taking God at his word? Then you need to hear the opening lines of Genesis 21:1–2: "Then the LORD took note of Sarah as He had said, and the LORD did for Sarah as He had promised. So Sarah conceived and bore a son to Abraham in his old age, at the appointed time of which God had spoken to him." Isn't that good to hear? It had been a long time coming, but God had not forgotten his promise to Sarah (17:19). God always does what he says he will do. He is not like us, forgetting, overlooking, and ignoring his commitments. Nor is he, like us, sometimes willing to fulfill his commitments, but unable to do so. He never runs out of time. He never gets sick, or has an unexpected scheduling conflict. And he never lacks the strength to do what he says he will do—even if the task is as tall as giving a baby to a ninety-year-old woman or raising his Son from the dead! Nothing is too hard for the Lord! And the Lord always does "as He had said."

Now read on into 21:3–4 and you will find that God wasn't the only one doing "as He had said"—so was Abraham! In verse 3, he named his new son Isaac, just as the LORD had instructed him back in 17:19. And in verse 4 we read that "Abraham circumcised his son Isaac when he was eight days old, as God had commanded him" in 17:10! — Kurt Strassner, *Opening up Genesis, Opening Up Commentary* (Leominster: Day One Publications, 2009), 90–91.

2. What is the mood of this passage? What is the emotion?

I am sure Abraham rejoiced too. But it is Sarah who properly leads the rejoicing. It was she who had been barren and who now, having at last conceived and given birth to Isaac, can hardly believe her good fortune or control her joy. Psalm 126 says, "When the Lord brought back the captives to Zion, we were like men who dreamed. Our mouths were filled with laughter, our tongues with songs of joy" (vv. 1-2). Sarah could have sung that song with variations. She could have said, "When the Lord brought back fertility to Sarah, I was like one who was dreaming. My mouth was filled with laughter and my tongue with songs of joy." I hear it as I read the passage. Sarah said, "God has brought me laughter [here she laughs], and everyone who hears about this will laugh with me." More laughter. "Who would have said to Abraham that Sarah would nurse children? [Here she squeezes Isaac so hard that he cries, and she covers him with kisses.] Yet I have borne him a son in his old age." She laughs again. — *Boice Expositional Commentary - An Expositional Commentary – Genesis, Volume 2: A New Beginning (Genesis 12-36).*

3. What do we learn about God from this story?

The reason for the joyful laughter of this passage, however, is not merely the birth of Isaac, though that is part of it. It is the delight of both Abraham and Sarah in God. God had done a great miracle, and his doing of it and the way he did it would be a source of joyful reflection and discussion by this great couple for years to come.

One lesson they learned is that God is faithful to his promise. They had believed God partially, but they had doubted him too. At times they had tried to take matters into their own hands, thinking that it was necessary for them to help God out. A year earlier, Sarah had utterly discounted the promise. But God was faithful in spite of human unbelief. This point is made clear by repetition. The passage says, "Now the Lord was gracious to Sarah as he had said, and the Lord did for Sarah what he had promised. Sarah became pregnant and bore a son to Abraham in his old age, at the very time God had promised him" (vv. 1-2, italics mine).

Has God made a promise to you? If he has, you may be sure he will keep it. You may waver, but he will not waver. You may disbelieve; he remains faithful. The day will come when you will laugh with joy at the fulfillment.

Second, these two individuals (Abraham and Sarah) learned that God is all-powerful. They learned that nothing is too hard for him. This too is emphasized in the passage; for just as God's keeping his word is stressed by a threefold repetition, so repetition is used to emphasize Abraham's age at the time of the birth: "Sarah... bore a son to Abraham in his old age.... Abraham was a hundred years old when his son Isaac was born to him.... Sarah said, 'I have borne him a son in his old age'" (vv. 2, 5, 7). Humanly speaking, there was no possibility at all that Abraham could have a child at this age. But although this was impossible with men, with God all things are possible. God is sovereign, and he can do what he will in his universe.

This is worth some reflection. When you and I read a passage like this, we tend to say, "Well, that was all right for Abraham and Sarah. God certainly did a miracle for them. But God can't do that for me. My situation is different. I am too old." Or, "Those who are opposing me are too strong." Let us face this for what it is: simple unbelief. Is God sovereign? Is God all-powerful? Then he can and will do what he has promised. I think this has special bearing in the matter of age. Some of us say that it is too late for God to work, that we are too old. But if the biblical record of Abraham's life is true—as it is— then we are never too old for God to do a new thing in us and with us. Moses was eighty when he began to lead the people of Israel out of Egypt, and he got in the modern equivalent (in years) of two full government careers (two times twenty years) before God finally retired him. As for Abraham, he lived seventy-five more years after the birth of Isaac, dying finally at the age of one hundred and seventy-five. Even if you are at the age of retirement, God may well have important work ahead for you to do.

Do not say, "But I don't have the strength to do it." God will give you whatever strength is necessary. I notice from this passage that God did not merely give Sarah the strength to conceive and bear a child. He gave her the ability to nurse the child too (v. 7). And Abraham did not receive strength to procreate merely one child. He was made "young" enough to father six more sons of his wife Keturah, whom he married after Sarah died (Gen. 25:1-2). One commentator has said, "When God miraculously heals, it is not a partial healing, but a complete and instant restoration." If God gives you a task, he will give you the strength and time you need to do it. — *Boice Expositional Commentary - An Expositional Commentary – Genesis, Volume 2: A New Beginning (Genesis 12-36).*

4. Verse 1 reminds us that God is a promise-keeping God. What are some of your favorite promises that you find yourself repeating to yourself?

God promised Abraham that He would make his descendants like the sands of the sea—uncountable. He did.

God promised Abraham that His people would go into slavery and he would lead them out. He did.

God promised Moses that He would use him to lead His people out of slavery. And He did.

God promised Joshua that He would use him to lead the people into the Promised Land. And He did.

God promised He would send a Savior and He did.

God promised He would send another Comforter in the person of the Holy Spirit. He did.

God promised He would prepare a place for us. He is. — Josh Hunt, Following God (Pulpit Press, 2015).

5. What do we learn about following God from this story?

A third lesson Abraham and Sarah learned, which is also emphasized in this account, is that God is in no hurry in carrying out his promises but rather has a set time for their fulfillment. The text says that "Sarah became pregnant and bore a son to Abraham in his old age, at the very time God had promised him" (v. 2). This time had been mentioned first in Genesis 17 ("My covenant I will establish with Isaac, whom Sarah will bear to you by this time next year," v. 21). It was reiterated twice in Genesis 18 ("I will surely return to you about this time next year, and Sarah your wife will have a son," v. 10; "I will return to you at the appointed time next year and Sarah will have a son," v. 14). Now the promise is fulfilled, and it is neither early nor late. It is "at the very time God had promised him."

One of the hardest things we face in life is what seems to us to be delays in God's actions. We pray. The answer is delayed. Then we fume and fret and sometimes set about to work out the answer for ourselves. What is wrong when we do this? Simply put: We are not trusting. We are doubting either God's ability to do what he has promised or God's timing. We need to trust God and wait upon him. — Boice Expositional Commentary - An Expositional Commentary – Genesis, Volume 2: A New Beginning (Genesis 12-36).

6. There was quite a gap in time between the promise given and the promise fulfilled. Is this normal when we follow God? Can you think of other examples?

And so at last we see the promise that was given to Abraham twenty-five years previously coming to pass. As we have noted, more often than not, there is a time gap between the promise and performance of God—a period which is invariably longer than we thought it would be, or than we think it should be. Because our implicit trust in the Lord will be a key ingredient in allowing us to function in the coming kingdom, it is essential that we be people of faith. So Abraham, the father of faith, was himself put into a place where his faith was stretched. — Jon Courson, *Jon Courson's Application Commentary: Volume One: Genesis–Job* (Nashville, TN: Thomas Nelson, 2005), 89.

7. Why does God often delay the answer to a prayer or the fulfillment of a promise?

Why does God delay in answering prayer? He wants to give us a better blessing. Why does God delay in bringing deliverance or healing? He has something better in store for us. Our times are in His hands.

We must remember that when we wait on the Lord, we are not being idle or careless. Waiting prepares us. God works in us so that He can work for us. He knows what He is doing and has His own schedule. "The Lord is not slack concerning His promise, as some [people] count slackness, but is longsuffering toward us, not willing that any should perish" (2 Pet. 3:9).

"Our heart shall rejoice in Him" (v. 21). Waiting ultimately leads to worship. The day will come when you will rejoice in the Lord because you have trusted in His holy name. "Let Your mercy, O LORD, be upon us, just as we hope in You" (v. 22). We have hope and faith in waiting on the Lord. If you find it hard to wait, remember that God's delays are not His denials. He has a greater blessing in store for you. You can be sure that one day the waiting will end, and you will start worshiping and praising Him. — Warren W. Wiersbe, *Prayer, Praise & Promises: A Daily Walk through the Psalms* (Grand Rapids, MI: Baker Books, 2011), 81.

8. What is God's agenda when He seems to delay? What is He up to?

Why does God delay answers to sincere prayers? It certainly is not because He lacks power. Moreover, He is most willing for us to receive from Him. No, the answer is found in this verse: "He spoke a parable to them, that men always ought to pray and not lose heart" (Luke 18:1).

The Greek word for lose heart means "to relax, become weak or weary in faith, give up the struggle, no longer wait for completion." Galatians 6:9 advises, "Let us not grow weary while doing good, for in due season we shall reap, if we do not lose heart."

The Lord is seeking a praying people who will not relax or grow weary of coming to Him. These will wait on the Lord, not giving up before His work is completed—and they will be found waiting when He brings the answer. — David Wilkerson, *God Is Faithful: A Daily Invitation into the Father Heart of God* (Grand Rapids, MI: Baker, 2012).

9. What good things happen to our hearts as we wait on God?

Why does God delay in bringing his promises to pass? Clearly, one reason is that we grow through suffering to maturity, learning patience through faith. If you are frustrated because God does not seem to be blessing you right now, confess your impatience. Think about the promises mentioned in this meditation. Ask the Spirit to call to your thinking other promises in Scripture. Thank God for riches now, and in due season. — R.C. Sproul, *Before the Face of God: Book 4: A Daily Guide for Living from Ephesians, Hebrews, and James, electronic ed.* (Grand Rapids: Baker Book House; Ligonier Ministries, 1994), 237.

10. Besides changing us, what other reason might there be for God to delay?

The first reason God delays, God is sometimes silent, is that it is always for His glory. God is always interested in bringing glory to Himself. If any of us were trying to do that, it would be supreme egotism. For any of us to try to get credit, to get glory, to be acclaimed, to be honored would be egotistical and inappropriate. But not for God, since He is perfect in beauty, perfect in holiness, perfect in grace, perfect in mercy. Everything about God is perfect. His provision is perfect, and everything that God does is designed to let people see the perfection that is His and to enter into that perfection through Jesus Christ. Nothing comes into our lives that God does not allow. When God allows silence to shroud our lives, when He delays in our lives, it is always for His glory. — James Draper, *Preaching with Passion: Sermons from the Heart of the Southern Baptist Convention* (Nashville: B&H, 2004).

11. Can you think of any ways that the birth of Isaac foreshadows the birth of Jesus?

The account of Isaac's birth would be a sufficient cause for joy just for the lessons I have mentioned—lessons undoubtedly learned by Abraham and Sarah. But for us there is even greater joy, because we see in this account a foreshadowing of Jesus' supernatural birth. This becomes quite obvious later on, when Abraham almost sacrifices his son and names the place where the sacrifice was made "The Lord Will Provide" (Gen. 22:14). This later incident directs us to Calvary. But taking that clue and then looking over the whole of Isaac's life, we find that he is a figure of Jesus at nearly every point.

Here are some parallels between Isaac's birth and that of Jesus. **First, Isaac and Jesus were both the promised seed and son.** We have seen this many times in the case of Isaac. In Jesus' case the promise was also freely given. Genesis 3:15 spoke of him: "I will put enmity between you and the woman, and between your offspring and hers; he will crush your head, and you will strike his heel." Isaiah 7:14 goes further: "The virgin will be with child and will give birth to a son, and will call him Immanuel." Hundreds of Old Testament prophecies look forward to the birth of Jesus, just as the promise to Abraham looked forward to the birth of his beloved son Isaac.

Second, there was a period of delay between the promises and their fulfillment. In Abraham's case, this was between twenty-five and thirty years, that is, from the time of his starting out from Ur until the birth of Isaac, when he was a hundred years old. In the case of Jesus, the delay was for hundreds, even thousands, of years.

Third, when Sarah heard the promise of Isaac's birth, she thought, "Will I really have a child, now that I am old?" (Gen. 18:13). God's answer to Sarah was: "Is anything too hard for the Lord?" (v. 14). We find something similar when the birth of Jesus was announced to Mary. Mary had greater faith than Sarah, but her question was about the same: "How will this be... since I am a virgin?" (Luke 1:34). The angel's response was: "Nothing is impossible with God" (v. 37). In each case, God answered with a statement of his own omnipotence.

Fourth, the names of the children were symbolic and were given before either was born. God told Abraham, "Your wife Sarah will bear you a son, and you will call him Isaac" (Gen. 17:19). God told Joseph, "She will give birth to a son, and you are to give him the name Jesus, because he will save his people from their sins" (Matt. 1:21).

Fifth, the births occurred at God's appointed time. Indeed, there is no parallel more striking than this. We have already seen how this element is emphasized in the birth of Isaac: "by this time next year" (Gen. 17:21), "about this time next year" (Gen. 18:10), "at the appointed time" (Gen. 18:14), "at the very time" (Gen. 21:2). In the same way, Paul says in Galatians 4:4, "But when the time had fully come, God sent his Son, born of a woman, born under law, to redeem those under law, that we might receive the full rights of sons." When the time had fully come! Like the birth of Isaac, the birth of Jesus was neither too early nor too late. It was at the time appointed by God. All the events of Christ's life likewise followed that previously determined plan.

Sixth, the birth of Jesus, like the birth of Isaac, required a miracle. It is strange in view of the miracle in Isaac's birth that so many of our contemporaries have denied it in the case of Jesus Christ. To be sure, the miracle in Jesus' birth was greater. It required conception without benefit of any human father, while in Isaac's case the miracle was only that of restoring reproductive power to an elderly couple. But this is what we should expect if the earlier birth is a foreshadowing of the later: a lesser miracle followed by a greater one. What is amazing is the tendency of so many to deny the later miracle. Yet miracle it was. By it, the dual nature of Jesus as both God and man was fully achieved and demonstrated.

Finally, there is the matter of laughter or joy, the theme with which we started. Sarah laughed. In Mary's case, we find nearly the same thing: "My soul glorifies the Lord and my spirit rejoices in God my Savior" (Luke 1:46-47). Nor was it only Mary who rejoiced at Jesus' birth. The angels also rejoiced and, in fact, invited others to rejoice too: "Do not be afraid. I bring you good news of great joy that will be for all the people. Today in the town of David a Savior has been born to you; he is Christ the Lord" (Luke 2:10-11).

The mirth surrounding Jesus' birth was not the mindless hilarity of the world, of course. But it was a real joy, analogous to the joy of Sarah at the birth of Isaac. Outwardly, the circumstances of Joseph, Mary, and the other people involved in Jesus' birth were far from good. Mary and Joseph were far from home, in a strange town, without even a room to themselves in which Mary could give birth to her child. If their laughter had depended on outward circumstances, there would have been very little of it on that occasion. But I am sure they laughed with joy. I think even the angels laughed. Why? Because that one who had been so long anticipated and whose birth had required such a wonderful miracle had finally come. The Savior was born. God was now with us. If you know Jesus to be that Savior, your own Savior from sin, then you understand that joy and share in it. You laugh in the joy of salvation. — *Boice Expositional Commentary - An Expositional Commentary – Genesis, Volume 2: A New Beginning (Genesis 12-36).*

2. How unusual is it for a woman to give birth at Sarah's age?

For many people, 13 children would be more than enough.

But not for Annegret Raunigk.

The 65-year-old German grandmother recently gave birth to quadruplets, making her the oldest woman ever to do so.

The new arrivals increase her progeny to a total of 17 children. And let's not forget her seven grandchildren.

Raunigk, a single mother, gave birth last week to three boys and one girl after a pregnancy of just under 26 weeks, the German broadcaster RTL reported.

The newborns -- whose names are Neeta, Dries, Bence and Fjonn -- were delivered by C-section and are being kept in incubators for premature babies, according to RTL. http://www.cnn.com/2015/05/24/europe/germany-grandmother-quadruplets/

13. Would you consider the birth of Isaac a miracle? Why or why not?

There are some very remarkable truths here that we need to lay hold of. First of all, the birth of Isaac was a miraculous birth. It was contrary to nature. In the fourth chapter of Romans, Paul writes that Abraham "... considered not his own body now dead ... neither yet the deadness of Sarah's womb" (Rom. 4:19). Out of death God brings forth life: this is a miraculous birth. We need to call attention to the fact that God did not flash the supernatural birth of Christ on the world as being something new. He began to prepare men for it, and therefore way back here at the birth of Isaac we have a miraculous birth.

We also find here that God had to deal with both Sarah and Abraham. They had to recognize that they could do nothing, that it would be impossible for them to have a child. Abraham is 100 years old; Sarah is 90 years old. In other words, the birth of Isaac must be a birth that they really have nothing to do with. — J. Vernon McGee, *Thru the Bible Commentary, electronic ed., vol. 1* (Nashville: Thomas Nelson, 1997), 86.

14. Verse 6. Can you think of another time when Sarah laughed?

There are times when it is very good to laugh, and this is one of them. For three chapters of Genesis (eight chapters of exposition) we have been dealing with one of the saddest and most sobering portions of the Word of God. Before this section, Genesis 17 portrayed God solemnly reaffirming his promise of the birth of a son to Abraham, but for three chapters of Genesis (eighty-nine verses) there has been nothing but one grim revelation or act after another: first, the announcement of Sodom's impending destruction; second, Abraham's ineffectual intercession for it; third, the deliverance of Lot and his family, followed by the destruction itself; fourth, Lot's sin with his daughters; and fifth, Abraham's shameful attempts to deceive Abimelech. These are all tragedies. So if there was ever a time to break out of gloom and into laughter, it is now—now, when Isaac, the son of promise, is finally born and Sarah says, "God has brought me laughter" (Gen. 21:6).

The name "Isaac" means "laughter." So it is interesting that laughter occurs at his birth. When Sarah at age eighty-nine had overheard the angels talking about her giving birth to Isaac the following year, she had laughed in unbelief (Gen. 18:12). When Abraham had heard God repeat the promise shortly before this, he had laughed in a kind of half-incredulous, half-believing acknowledgment of God's truthfulness (Gen. 17:17). Now, however, the laughter is believing, spontaneous, and uncontrolled. For Isaac has been born. The son of the promise has been given. — *Boice Expositional Commentary - An Expositional Commentary – Genesis, Volume 2: A New Beginning* (Genesis 12-36).

15. Why do you think she laughed? What was she thinking? What was she feeling?

Finally, fourteen years later, when Abram is pushing a century of years and Sarai ninety ... when Abram has stopped listening to Sarai's advice, and Sarai has stopped giving it ... when the wallpaper in the nursery is faded and the baby furniture is several seasons out of date ... when the topic of the promised child brings sighs and tears and long looks into a silent sky ... God pays them a visit and tells them they had better select a name for their new son.

Abram and Sarai have the same response: laughter. They laugh partly because it is too good to happen and partly because it might. They laugh because they have given up hope, and hope born anew is always funny before it is real.

They laugh at the lunacy of it all.

Abram looks over at Sarai—toothless and snoring in her rocker, head back and mouth wide open, as fruitful as a pitted prune and just as wrinkled. And he cracks up. He tries to contain it, but he can't. He has always been a sucker for a good joke.

Sarai is just as amused. When she hears the news, a cackle escapes before she can contain it. She mumbles something about her husband's needing a lot more than what he's got and then laughs again.

They laugh because that is what you do when someone says he can do the impossible. They laugh a little at God, and a lot with God—for God is laughing, too. Then, with the smile still on his face, he gets busy doing what he does best—the unbelievable. — Max Lucado, *The Applause of Heaven* (Dallas, TX: Word Pub., 1996), 38–39.

16. Is it important that we laugh, or does it matter?

The late Norman Cousins, formerly editor of Saturday Review, had so serious a disease in the 1960's that doctors gave him only one in five hundred chances of surviving. That gaunt prediction notwithstanding, he beat the odds by rejecting hospital treatment and formulating his own plan. He took massive doses of vitamin C, watched Marx Brothers films and Candid Camera reruns, and read exhaustively from humor books. He found that laughter banished negative feelings and relieved his pain. Previously, pain led to tension and tension to more pain. He discovered that ten minutes of "genuine belly laughter" gave him at least two hours of pain-free sleep.

Gelotology—the science of humor—is in its infancy and cannot explain all the reasons laughter is so valuable to us. Perhaps it relieves pain by releasing endorphins, the body's natural opiates, into the bloodstream. It certainly protects us from negative emotions and attitudes. It encourages us to develop self-enhancing behavior patterns.

While humor encouraged better health for Mr. Cousins, it was still a limited benefit. Christ offers an eternal benefit. He removes sin from our lives altogether, absolutely, completely, and forever. In Christ, God claims complete amnesia over the sins we have committed and confessed. For good reason. Jesus had the perfect sacrifice to offer: himself He had the place to offer it: the cross. He had a compelling reason to offer it: forgiveness. He had a place to take it once offered: into heaven. He had a purpose in taking it there: to represent us eternally before the throne of God. — Virgil Hurley, *Speaker's Sourcebook of New Illustrations, electronic ed.* (Dallas: Word Publishers, 2000), 106–107.

17. Proverbs 17:22. How literally do you take this? Do you think that a cheerful heart is like medicine?

It is a proven fact of modern health science that a person's mental and spiritual health is strongly correlated with physical health. — *Defender's Study Bible*

18. What good things come to those who laugh?

A little laughter can go a long way, a new study reveals.

We all know the mood-boosting benefits of a good laugh, but researchers at California's Loma Linda University set out to find out if humor can deliver more than just comic relief. The study looked at 20 healthy older adults in their 60s and 70s, measuring their stress levels and short-term memory. One group was asked to sit silently, not talking, reading, or using their cellphones, while the other group watched funny videos.

After 20 minutes, the participants gave saliva samples and took a short memory test. While both groups performed better after the break than before, the "humor group" performed significantly better when it came to memory recall. Participants who viewed the funny videos had much higher improvement in recall abilities, 43.6 percent, compared with 20.3 percent in the non-humor group.

Moreover, the humor group showed considerably lower levels of cortisol, the "stress hormone," after watching the videos. The non-humor group's stress levels decreased just slightly.

Other studies have also shown the wide-ranging health benefits of laughter. A Vanderbilt University study estimated that just 10-15 minutes of laughter a day can burn up to 40 calories. Meanwhile, a University of Maryland study found that a sense of humor can protect against heart disease.

Lower cortisol? Lower stress? Sounds pretty good. But researchers insist the benefits are even greater.

"There are several benefits to humor and laughter," explained Gurinder S. Bains, a Ph.D. candidate at Loma Linda University, who co-authored the study. "Older adults need to have a better quality of life. Incorporating time to laugh, through social interaction with friends, enjoying exercise in a group setting, or even watching 20 minutes of humor on TV daily, can enhance your learning ability and delayed recall."
http://www.huffingtonpost.com/2014/04/22/laughter-and-memory_n_5192086.html

19. Abraham was 100 years old when he started rearing the child of promise. Have you ever felt you are too old to do anything for God? What would you say to a friend who said he thought he was too old to do anything for God?

You are never too old for God to work in your life. You are never too old to turn to God. You are never too old to follow God with your whole heart.

Abraham was a hundred years old when his son Isaac was born to him. Genesis 21:5

One hundred years old. That is old. But not too old for God to work. You are never too old for God to work.

C. S. Lewis said, "You are never too old to set another goal or to dream a new dream."

The American dream is to retire early with plenty of money, move to Florida, play golf and collect sea shells. That is not God's dream. He still has something for me to do.

Moses was eighty years old when God called him at the burning bush. Eighty years old was not too old. It was time to go to work; it was time to get started on his life's call. He has spent 40 years imagining God was through with him. God showed up. It was time to go to work. — Josh Hunt, *Following God* (Pulpit Press, 2015).

20. Summary. What does this story teach us about the sovereignty of God?

AT LONG LAST, at the appointed time, Abraham and Sarah received the fulfillment of God's promise. Ninety-year-old Sarah gave birth to a son and, in obedience to God, named him Isaac, which means "he laughs." Years earlier, when God had told Abraham that Sarah would give birth to a son, he fell over laughing. When God came again to announce, "I will return to you about this time next year, and your wife, Sarah, will have a son!" (Genesis 18:10), Sarah, too, laughed in disbelief. She was the age of most great-grandmothers by that time. Neither she nor Abraham could imagine her birthing and nursing her own infant.

When God accomplished the impossible through this aging couple, their disbelieving snickering became joyful laughter . . . laughter of pleasure and praise. They now saw greater meaning in the name Isaac.

Nothing occurs outside God's plan, and everything happens exactly at the time He planned it to happen. That's what theologians mean when they apply the term sovereignty to God. He has a plan, and He has the power and the will to carry it out.

Some people don't like the concept of sovereignty and the existence of a foreordained, divine plan. It makes them feel unimportant, as though they don't have a say in their own destiny. But God's foreordained plan does not reduce us to robots who must follow a program.

We grow up when we look at God's plan not as something that diminishes humanity by taking away our free will but as a means by which He will restore true freedom —and carry out His impossible plans. — Charles R. Swindoll, *Faith for the Journey: Daily Meditations on Courageous Trust in God* (Carol Stream, IL: Tyndale, 2014).

21. How can we maintain patience when God seems to be taking a long time?

LONG AFTER Abraham and Sarah had given up hope of experiencing this joy, they held their very own son in their arms. It would have been easy for them to lose hope when the fulfillment of the promise didn't come about in the way or the timing they expected. But their trust in the Lord went deeper than their human perspective, deeper than their doubts.

As I look back on my life, I recall many prayers I'm thankful the Lord chose to set aside. He gave me instead what I needed. And what He gave brought me even greater long-term happiness and more deep-down joy.

But when we're in the midst of a trial or a time of waiting, it can be difficult to have that perspective. What can we do when we find ourselves in such a season?

First, we can ask the Lord for sustaining strength and divine wisdom. I know that sounds elementary, but we often forget that we can't do life on our own. We need divine help from one day to the next. In addition, we need supernatural strength and divine wisdom to wait for God's plan to unfold. Good things come to those who wait.

Second, we can forgive yourself for being shortsighted and for missing the big picture. Forgive yourself for clinging when you should have released. Forgive yourself for failing to be excited about what's ahead when God's plan doesn't include your plans. Repent of your failings, receive God's forgiveness, and then forgive yourself.

I've learned this in my lifetime: the last one we forgive on this earth is ourselves. God forgives you, so why don't you?

In time, you will come to realize, as Abraham did, that in God's appointed plan, the best is yet to come. — Charles R. Swindoll, *Faith for the Journey: Daily Meditations on Courageous Trust in God* (Carol Stream, IL: Tyndale, 2014).

22. How can we support one another in prayer this week?

True prayer belongs in the small group because its effects are enhanced in community. It allows a group to learn more about God. Small group prayer also helps people know each other better.

When we share communication with God, we are also communicating with each other. In prayer our greatest desires often pour forth. We exchange, with God and each other, our vision, love for God, and motivation to follow God. Listening to a new believer pray is like receiving a breath of fresh air. Hearing a mature believer converse with the master is a rich experience. Sharing prayer with teachers, young mothers, teens, construction workers, and other kinds of persons, helps you understand their world much better.

Small group prayer also gives structure to the rejoicing, suffering body of Christ spoken of in 1 Corinthians 12. It is hard to get a fellowship of 80—or 250 or 1,000—to identify intimately with your struggles and joys. It is much easier to share together in prayer with a group of six close friends. People who share prayer needs and joys in a small group are loved and cared for. — Jeffrey Arnold and Stephanie Black, *The Big Book on Small Groups* (Downers Grove, IL: InterVarsity Press, 1992).

Genesis, Lesson #12
Good Questions Have Small Groups Talking
www.joshhunt.com

Genesis 22.1 - 14

OPEN

Let's each your name and how many kids and grandkids do you have?

DIG

1. Let's look at this story as a whole. What New Testament truths do you see pictured in this story?

The heart of the Christian faith is about substitutionary atonement. One payment is substituted for another.

> I owed a debt I could not pay.
> He paid a debt He did not owe.

That is substitutionary atonement. It is pictured in this story. Notice the word "instead."

> Abraham looked up and there in a thicket he saw a ram caught by its horns. He went over and took the ram and sacrificed it as a burnt offering instead of his son. Genesis 22:13

Christ lived a sinless life, yet was punished like a common criminal. That is not exactly right. He was punished like an extraordinarily bad criminal. We reserve capital punishment for the worst of criminals. That is how He died. That is how He was punished. The punishment was what we deserved. He did it for us. He did it instead of us.

Accept the gift of God's substitutionary atonement. Accept His righteousness in place of your guilt. — Josh Hunt, Following God (Pulpit Press, 2015).

2. What is the tone of this story? What is the emotion? What background music do you hear playing—if any?

Of all that sadnesses that can break our heart, perhaps the saddest is losing a child.

I have had my heart broken, but never like that. I can't think of anything as painful as losing a child.

If you ever have to stand by a friend who loses a child, don't say anything stupid. Don't say you understand.

God asked Abraham to give up his child. How sad. And this was not any child—this was the child of promise that he had waited for his whole life. God asked him to give him up. How unspeakably sad.

But, like any good leader, God leads by example. He never asks us to do what He Himself is not willing to do. He was not just willing—He actually did give up the life of His child. He asked Abraham to be willing. In the final seconds, He stayed his hand. When it was Jesus on the altar, no one stayed the Father's hand.

If you have lost a child, I don't know what to say, except perhaps this: we serve a God who knows what it is to give up the life of a Child. — Josh Hunt, *Following God* (Pulpit Press, 2015).

3. This is a familiar story for many of us. How did Abraham experience it differently than we do as we read it?

This isn't a movie. As far as Abraham was concerned, the drama didn't have a surprise ending. The knife goes up in order to bring it down into his son's chest or across his throat, and what will happen next is the death of his boy. This is real!

This is faith in the wild where the stakes are incredibly high—life and death!

Suddenly, at the last possible moment, God intervened:

> But the angel of the LORD called to him from heaven and said, "Abraham, Abraham!" And he said, "Here I am." He said, "Do not stretch out your hand against the lad, and do nothing to him; for now I know that you fear God, since you have not withheld your son, your only son, from Me." (Genesis 22:11–12)

As the Lord stopped Abraham's hand midplunge, He said, in effect, "You've passed the test, My faithful friend. You've proven to Me who is first, My aging son. You have also proven that your faith has reached full maturity. Your willingness to give up your only son has demonstrated that while you love the gift, you love the Giver more."

> Then Abraham raised his eyes and looked, and behold, behind him a ram caught in the thicket by his horns; and Abraham went and took the ram, and offered him up for a burnt offering in the place of his son. And Abraham called the name of that place The LORD Will Provide, as it is said to this day, "In the mount of the LORD it will be provided." (vv. 13–14)

After this, hundreds of years and ancient sands have covered the site. However, this very mountaintop would one day accommodate a city and a temple. It would become the capital of God's covenant kingdom and His house of worship until, finally, it would be the place where Christ, the King and consummate sacrifice, would die. Moriah, Jerusalem, the place where another Father held His Son loosely, laid Him on an altar, and sacrificed Him for us. On this mountain in the region of Moriah—a place renamed "The Lord will provide"—a ram became Isaac's substitute, and Christ became ours. — Charles R. Swindoll, *Great Days with the Great Lives* (Nashville: Thomas Nelson, 2006).

4. Locate Moriah on a map. What is significant about this location?

Moriah literally means "Foreseen of Jehovah." Therefore, it is as if God is saying, "Take your son, your only son, where you will provide a sneak preview of coming attractions." You see, God would sacrifice His only Son on the same spot to which He called Abraham. — Jon Courson, *Jon Courson's Application Commentary: Volume One: Genesis–Job* (Nashville, TN: Thomas Nelson, 2005), 102.

5. Verse 1. Why? Why did God test Abraham?

When pain comes our way, we always ask the same question: Why? Somehow, we think if we have a big enough "Why" we can handle the pain.

Why did God ask Abraham to slay his son? Swindoll offers some insight:

> Why? Why would a good and loving God ask an obedient and faithful man to do this? The answer can be found in the original language of Moses, the inspired, human author of Genesis. The Hebrew word nasah, translated "tested" in Genesis 22:1, has the idea of proving the quality of something, usually by putting it through a trial of some kind. God wanted to prove the validity—the authenticity—of Abraham's faith.

One question remains: prove to whom? Certainly not to God. He knows all things. Do you suppose Abraham had any doubts about himself? After two recorded lies—who knows how many more—do you think Abraham had any self-doubt? After attempting to fulfill the promise through Hagar, do you think he had any self-doubt?

God wanted to affirm Abraham, so He tested him. From time to time, He will test us as well. — Josh Hunt, *Following God* (Pulpit Press, 2015).

6. Does God test us at times? Has God ever tested you? Who has a story?

Why? Why would a good and loving God ask an obedient and faithful man to do this? The answer can be found in the original language of Moses, the inspired, human author of Genesis. The Hebrew word nasah, translated "tested" in Genesis 22:1, has the idea of proving the quality of something, usually by putting it through a trial of some kind. God wanted to prove the validity—the authenticity—of Abraham's faith.

Remember, though, that God is omniscient. He knows all things, including the future. He knew the heart of Abraham better than Abraham did. The purpose of the test was not to satisfy God's curiosity. This was not an experiment. The appointed patch of ground at the top of a lonely mountain in the land of Moriah was to be Abraham's proving ground. This would be the time and place where any question about his faltering faith—so evident in his lying (twice) to save his skin and his pathetic attempt to fulfill the covenant through his wife's handmaid—would be put to rest. His family would see his faith, his friends would see it, we would see it by virtue of this record, and probably most important of all, Isaac would see it. If ever faith would be put on display, this would be the day.

The issue in question: Did Abraham love the gift of God or God Himself?

Allow me to put Abraham's test on hold and rush into the twenty-first century. This has to be one of the toughest questions any parent has to consider: Do I adore the gifts God gives me more than I adore the Giver? Have I begun to worship the relationships that God has granted me rather than the One who gave me these delights?

Don't be too quick to answer.

The word worship comes from an Anglo-Saxon term meaning "worthship." When we worship something, we are affirming its value to us. We do that with our actions as well as with our hearts. A parent must ask, Do I assign more worth to my child than I do my God? To answer that question, follow the trail of your sacrifices. Tally the results. Be painfully honest now. For whom do you sacrifice more—or more often? — Charles R. Swindoll, *Great Days with the Great Lives* (Nashville: Thomas Nelson, 2006).

7. Why does God test His children?

Why? Why would a good and loving God ask an obedient and faithful man to do this? The answer can be found in the original language of Moses, the inspired, human author of Genesis. The Hebrew word nasah, translated "tested" in Genesis 22:1, has the idea of proving the quality of something, usually by putting it through a trial of some kind. God wanted to prove the validity—the authenticity—of Abraham's faith.

Remember, though, that God is omniscient. He knows all things, including the future. He knew the heart of Abraham better than Abraham did. The purpose of the test was not to satisfy God's curiosity. This was not an experiment. The appointed patch of ground at the top of a lonely mountain in the land of Moriah was to be Abraham's proving ground. This would be the time and place where any question about his faltering faith—so evident in his lying (twice) to save his skin and his pathetic attempt to fulfill the covenant through his wife's handmaid—would be put to rest. His family would see his faith, his friends would see it, we would see it by virtue of this record, and probably most important of all, Isaac would see it. If ever faith would be put on display, this would be the day.

The issue in question: Did Abraham love the gift of God or God Himself?

Allow me to put Abraham's test on hold and rush into the twenty-first century. This has to be one of the toughest questions any parent has to consider: Do I adore the gifts God gives me more than I adore the Giver? Have I begun to worship the relationships that God has granted me rather than the One who gave me these delights? — Charles R.

Swindoll, *Great Days with the Great Lives* (Nashville: Thomas Nelson, 2006).

8. Genesis 22.2. Does this remind you of a New Testament verse?

One of the many things that amazes me about the Bible is how it weaves together as a whole. Here is a large book written by forty people on three continents over 2000 years and it all fits together as a whole.

No one who has read the New Testament can read Genesis 22 without thinking of John 3:16.

- Then God said, "Take your son, your only son, whom you love—Isaac—and go to the region of Moriah. Sacrifice him there as a burnt offering on a mountain I will show you." Genesis 22:2

- For God so loved the world that He gave His one and only Son, that whoever believes in Him shall not perish but have eternal life. John 3:16

And this is not just a literary coincidence. This is the heart of the message of the Bible. God sent His son as the sacrifice for our sins. Two thousand years before that, this was pictured by God asking Abraham to give up his son, his only son.

Oh, did I mention this happened on the same range of mountains?

There is a big difference in the two stories. In the Abraham story, the Father stayed Abraham's hand at the last minute and his son was spared. On Golgotha, no one stayed the Father's hand.

Pray a silent prayer of gratitude just now. — Josh Hunt, *Following God* (Pulpit Press, 2015).

9. What other similarities do you see between Isaac and Jesus?

Isaac is a picture, a type of Christ...

- Conceived miraculously when a heretofore-barren Sarah was ninety years old, Isaac was a miracle baby.

- Born of a virgin, Jesus was a miracle Baby.

- Isaac's birth was promised long before he showed up—twenty years before he was born.

- Jesus' birth was promised clear back in Genesis 3:15—approximately 4,000 years before His birth in Bethlehem.

- Abraham and Sarah were told what to name their son.

- Mary and Joseph were told what to name their Son.

- To his father, Isaac was obedient to the point of death.

- To His Father, Jesus was obedient to death.

The parallels are many. Isaac and Jesus are linked together. Isaac is the type; Jesus the fulfillment. — Jon Courson, *Jon Courson's Application Commentary: Volume One: Genesis–Job* (Nashville, TN: Thomas Nelson, 2005), 101.

10. Imagine. What thoughts might have gone through Abraham's head as he contemplated giving up Isaac?

The command to go and offer Isaac as a sacrifice would have seemed totally unreasonable to Abraham. The pagans may have offered human sacrifice, but it was out of harmony with the nature of God. Beyond that, how could God fulfill the promises he had made earlier if the promised seed was now to be destroyed? And at Abraham's age there would not likely be another child, at least not one through Sarah. The cost to the covenant would be enormous, not to mention the emotional loss to Abraham and Sarah. — Allen Ross and John N. Oswalt, *Cornerstone Biblical Commentary: Genesis, Exodus, vol. 1* (Carol Stream, IL: Tyndale House Publishers, 2008), 141–142.

11. Genesis 22.3. What do you admire about Abraham from this verse?

I think I would have procrastinated. I would have slept in. Or, maybe I couldn't sleep, (who could?) but I would delay setting off. Abraham got up and left: "Early the next morning Abraham got up and loaded his donkey. He took with him two of his servants and his son Isaac. When he had cut enough wood for the burnt offering, he set out for the place God had told him about." Genesis 22:3

The Navigators would site this as an example of instant obedience. They like to say that anything less than instant obedience is disobedience. Abraham got up early and left. First thing in the morning. No delay. No hesitation. No lolly-gagging.

God is looking for people of instant obedience. People who jump when God say says jump.

Perhaps you have been feeling God's leading to do something. Perhaps that is why you bought this book. Perhaps it is time to get with it.

There is a time for prayerful consideration and there is a time to act. — Josh Hunt, *Following God* (Pulpit Press, 2015).

12. Genesis 22.4. Do a search on your smart phone for the phrase, "third day." How many times can you find it in the Bible?

On the third day Abraham looked up and saw the place in the distance. Genesis 22:4

The phrase, "third day" appears no less than forty-one times in the Bible. If we expand the search to include the phrase, "three days" the number swells to one hundred and five.

It is as if God is saying, "Pay attention to the third day. Important things happen on the third day." Ortberg says:

The Old Testament Scriptures are filled with what might be called "third-day stories." When Abraham is afraid he's going to have to sacrifice Isaac, he sees the sacrifice that will save his son's life on the third day. Joseph's brothers get put in prison, and they're released on the third day. Israelite spies are told by Rahab to hide from their enemies, and then they'll be safe on the third day. When Esther hears that her people are going to be slaughtered, she goes away to fast and pray. On the third day, the king receives her favorably.

The most important third day story of all:

> For what I received I passed on to you as of first importance: that Christ died for our sins according to the Scriptures, that He was buried, that He was raised on the third day according to the Scriptures. 1 Corinthians 15:3–4

Josh Hunt, *Following God* (Pulpit Press, 2015).

13. Verse 5. What do we learn about worship from this story?

Abraham is about to sacrifice his only son—and what word does he use to describe the act? "Worship." He's headed up the mountain to place the biggest part of his life on an altar and he calls it "Worship."

When we think of worship we typically think of offering a song, or a prayer, or a gift. But when Abraham worshiped, he offered his son. He offered the biggest part of his life to God. — Max Lucado, *Everyday Blessings: Inspirational Thoughts from the Published Works of Max Lucado.* (Nashville, TN: Thomas Nelson, Inc., 2004).

14. What do you think Abraham has in mind when he says that we will be right back?

Abraham's response was almost as amazing as the test: He responded with instant, unquestioning obedience to the command of God. He even got an early start! However, the three-day journey (22:4) probably became more and more difficult as he drew near to the place, for the Hebrew narrative slows down the action with a more deliberate manner of telling the story (using more ands than needed—a rhetorical device called polysyndeton). When Abraham saw the place in the region of Moriah, he took only Isaac with him and left the two servants and the donkey behind. He said, "We will worship there, and then we will come right back" (22:5). This could also be translated, "We will worship there in order that we may return." His statement is amazing, and raises all kinds of questions regarding what was going through his mind at this moment. All that Abraham knew was that God had planned the future of the covenant around Isaac and that God wanted him to sacrifice Isaac. He could not reconcile these two things in his own mind, but could only do what God commanded him to do, leaving the future to God. That is faith. — Allen Ross and John N. Oswalt, *Cornerstone Biblical Commentary: Genesis, Exodus, vol. 1* (Carol Stream, IL: Tyndale House Publishers, 2008), 142.

15. What quality in Abraham do you admire in verse 8?

In response to Isaac's question, "Where is the sheep for the burnt offering?" (22:7), Abraham again revealed his faith in the Lord, "God will provide a sheep for the burnt offering, my son" (22:8). This statement of Abraham's would become the motive for the naming to follow (see 22:14 and note) and the theme of the entire narrative for the household of faith.

God's intervention was dramatic and instructive; it revealed that he had never intended for the boy to be sacrificed; child sacrifice was never to be practiced in Israel. What God wanted from Abraham was actually for Abraham to sacrifice his own will, to surrender his will to God by giving up his dearest possession. And when that happened, God intervened. So in a way Isaac was brought from the dead twice, once from the dead womb of Sarah by divine intervention, and once from the altar where he was essentially sacrificed to God (Heb 11:17–19). The angel of the Lord stopped Abraham just as he was ready to plunge the knife into his son (22:10–11). God then knew that Abraham would hold nothing back from him, that he did in fact fear God (22:12). This usage harmonizes with the biblical meaning, for to fear God means to revere him as sovereign, trust him implicitly, and obey him without question or protest. — Allen Ross and John N. Oswalt, *Cornerstone Biblical Commentary: Genesis, Exodus, vol. 1* (Carol Stream, IL: Tyndale House Publishers, 2008), 142.

16. Genesis 22.10. What do we learn about following God from Abraham's example?

Abraham was not a perfect man. He lied about Sarah. He went along with Sarah's plan to sleep with Hagar. When God said he would have a son, he laughed out loud. There is a lot to be critical about with Abraham.

But, in this shining moment, Abraham shows what it means to be a mature God-follower. When God placed His hand on the most precious thing in Abraham' life, Abraham willingly surrendered. "I surrender all" was more than a song.

Imagine it. Raising your knife over your son—the son of promise. Imagine the look of terror in your son's eyes. Imagine your son shrieks, "Why are you doing this? I thought you loved me?" What do you say?

This is obedience. This is discipleship. This is what it means to follow God. It means to follow when it is hard. It means to follow when you don't understand. It means to follow when it doesn't make any sense at all. It means to follow when your heart is broken.

Mark it down; when you follow God, your heart will be broken. You won't always understand. It won't always make sense.

And yet, you follow. That is what Abraham did. That is what we must do. — Josh Hunt, *Following God* (Pulpit Press, 2015).

17. Verse 9. What was this day like for Isaac? How did he experience it?

Some people live so carefully they absolutely refuse to take risks. Everything has to be carefully regulated and kept under control . . . their control. Borders defined, guidelines spelled out, every dime accounted for, no surprises. And after having expended so much time and effort trying to live safely, they end life never having accomplished anything of lasting value. They built nothing, tried nothing new, invested in no one.

Not Abraham! His faith had matured to the point that his absolute confidence in God's character gave him the freedom to throw caution to the wind and risk everything to obey. What a perfect lesson in theology for his son.

Now, Abraham didn't raise a fool for a son. Isaac could piece all the clues together. He does that as the story continues. We read that they came to the place of which God had told him. Abraham built the altar there, arranged the wood, and then bound Isaac and laid him on the altar.

I've heard this passage preached countless times, and I've never heard anyone talk about the quiet faith of this remarkable young man. He's the sacrifice, yet he allowed himself to be bound up and placed onto that altar! Obviously, this son learned his theology well from his father—a father who released his son because he completely trusted his God. By the way, Isaac didn't learn such faith on his way up the mountain that morning. He'd been cultivating it over the years, thanks to his father who modeled it often.

Some of you parents may find yourselves in a similar situation as you read these pages. Your relationship with your child may have reached a point where you have no other choice but to commit him or her completely to God's care. You would love to work out the details, but you cannot. You know the Lord is good, and you have prayed for a resolution, but nothing has changed. Only God can intervene. And because that is true, you can take your cues from Abraham.

Place your relationship with that son or daughter on the altar today. Surrender him or her to the Lord as an offering. Take this risk. Mentally place your boy or girl on top of the wood, and step back from the altar. Trust God. In His time, He will provide. — Charles R. Swindoll, *Great Days with the Great Lives* (Nashville: Thomas Nelson, 2006).

18. This passage begins by saying the Lord tested Abraham. What kind of grade do you give Abraham on this test?

Abraham passed his test with flying colors, and so did Moses. In fact, Moses offered himself in the place of his people—even willing to give up his hope of heaven if God would spare them.

Moses said to the Lord: "Oh, what a great sin these people have committed! They have made themselves gods of gold. But now, please forgive their sin—but if not, then blot me out of the book you have written" (Exodus 32:31-32, NIV).

This pleased the Lord, and He spared them. By offering himself as a sacrifice for a sinful nation, Moses was actually foreshadowing Jesus, who would give His life as a ransom for the world. And I can imagine God saying to him, "Moses, you remind Me of My Son."

Moses had come such a long way from the impetuous young Prince of Egypt, or the passive old man in the desert, watching the bush burn. He was now God's man, God's intercessor, and God's friend. He was beloved of the Lord. — Greg Laurie, *The Greatest Stories Ever Told, Volume One* (Dana Point, CA: Kerygma Publishing—Allen David Books, 2011).

19. Summary. What do we learn about God from this passage? What do we learn about following God?

This passage not only records the great test of Abraham, the pinnacle of his life of faith, but it also sets forth the pattern for sacrificial worship down through the ages. Like Abraham, a true worshiper of God holds nothing back from God, but obediently gives him what he asks, trusting that God will provide all his needs. A true worshiper knows that everything belongs to God anyway—it all came from God, and therefore must be acknowledged as God's own possession. The key idea of the whole passage is summarized in the commemorative name that Abraham gave to the place: "The LORD will provide" or "The LORD will see to it" (yhwh yir'eh [3068/7200, 3378/8011]; see note on 22:14). This truth is at the heart of faithful worship: The Lord was to be worshiped by his people on his holy mountain. Three times a year the people were to appear (yera'eh [7200, 8011], "be seen") before the Lord to worship him, bringing their sacrifices and offerings to him (Exod 23:17; Deut 16:16). They were to bring to God the best sacrifice they had, trusting that he would continue to provide for their needs—but they had to offer the sacrifice to God first and then expect his provision. Thus, they went to the sanctuary to "see" (ra'ah) the Lord, to behold his power and glory in the way he answered prayers and provided for his people (Ps 63:2–5). And God would "see" (ra'ah) the needs of those who came before him with their sacrifices, and would bless them with provisions for life. Thus in providing for them he would be seen. So a motto grew up for Israel's worship: "On the mountain of the LORD it will be seen" (or "it will be provided," or "he will be seen"; see note on 22:14). Faith first surrenders the dearest and the best to God, believing that God will provide.

In naming the place Abraham was commemorating his own experience of sacrifice to the Lord. But an animal (a ram, not a "sheep"; 22:8), caught by its horns in a thornbush, was the divine provision for the sacrifice. By his grace God allowed Abraham to offer a substitute sacrifice, an animal in the place of Isaac (22:13). Later all Israel would offer animals to the Lord, knowing that God's grace had provided for a substitute sacrifice to be made for the worshiper. Out of this event, Israel developed a major theological teaching: Whenever an animal was offered on the holy mountain of God, God remembered Isaac (this is seen in rabbinic writings on the Akedah). In other words, the believer knew that the sacrifice he was offering was a substitute, and that the true sacrifice that was pleasing to God was a broken heart, his heart broken of self-will and surrendered to God. And that surrender would be expressed by offering the best that could be given to God.

The passage also anticipates God's substituting his only son for all humanity, making the perfect sacrifice once and for all. John certainly had this in mind when he introduced Jesus as the Lamb of God who takes away the sin of the world (John 1:29). Yet the focus of Genesis 22 is not on the doctrine of atonement. Rather, it is portraying an obedient servant worshiping God in faith at great cost and then receiving God's provision. Abraham did not withhold his son from God. Similarly Paul wrote that God "did not spare (epheisato [5339, 5767]) even his own Son but gave him up for us all" (Rom 8:32). A form of the same word is used in the Greek version of Genesis 22:12: "You have not spared (epheisō) your beloved son." And based on this motif, Paul gets to the point, both of Genesis 22 and of his own argument: "Won't he also give us everything else?" If God gave us the dearest possession he has, he will surely provide all things for us. — Allen Ross and John N. Oswalt, *Cornerstone Biblical Commentary: Genesis, Exodus, vol. 1* (Carol Stream, IL: Tyndale House Publishers, 2008), 142–143.

20. How can we support one another in prayer this week?

Genesis, Lesson #13
Good Questions Have Small Groups Talking
www.joshhunt.com

Email your group and ask them to do a little reading about discovering the will of God.

Genesis 24.1 - 17

OPEN
Let's each your name and what is the next trip you have planned?

DIG
1. **Overview. What do we learn about following God from this story?**

   In Genesis 24, the structure of this twice-told story of Isaac and Rebekah gives us the advantage of knowing what happens before the main characters do and thereby observing the providential workings of God in everyday life. The position of this great story in Genesis at the end of Abraham's life serves, in effect, to tell us that this is the way God works day in and day out in our lives. Such a God, of course, is great beyond our imaginings because he maintains all of life, involves himself in all events, and directs all things to their appointed end while rarely interrupting the natural order of life.

   This is an awesome thought. The God of Scripture is not simply a God of miracles who occasionally injects his power into life. He is far greater because he arranges all of life to suit and effect his providence. This makes all of life a miracle. God is over all. He is all-powerful, all-knowing, all-present, and all-controlling. This is the God of Scripture. Anything less is an idolatrous reduction of our puny imaginations. — R. Kent Hughes, *Genesis: Beginning and Blessing, Preaching the Word* (Wheaton, IL: Crossway Books, 2004), 316–317.

2. Verse 2. What do we know about this servant?

We must also take careful note that Abraham's servant was also himself a man of remarkable faith and, as Derek Kidner says, one of the most attractive minor characters of the Bible. If this was Eliezer of Damascus, he had been at one time a potential heir of Abraham, who had been now displaced by the birth of Abraham's sons (cf. Genesis 15:2). In character he was like the future John the Baptist who declared, "He must increase, but I must decrease" (John 3:30). So it was with profound covenantal faith that the servant obediently placed his hand under Abraham's thigh (v. 9) and swore in magnificent oath "by the LORD, the God of heaven and God of the earth" (v. 3) that he would carry out Abraham's wishes. — R. Kent Hughes, *Genesis: Beginning and Blessing, Preaching the Word* (Wheaton, IL: Crossway Books, 2004), 317.

3. Where was "my country"? Where was Abraham sending this servant?

This event emphasizes the providence of God through the faithfulness of the people to bring about the marriage of Isaac and Rebekah. Abraham, confident in the Lord's promise, had his chief servant swear to find a wife from Abraham's relatives back east, some 450 miles away. Eliezer's putting his hand underAbraham's thigh (24:2; cf. 47:29) was a solemn oath that he would find a bride for Isaac so that the seed could be continued to the next generation. Taking the oath put the burden on the servant to complete the commission. If the woman he found was not willing to return with him, then he was free from the oath. But by no means was he to take Isaac out of the land in the process. Abraham was thereby ensuring that Isaac would be safe, both physically and in terms of perpetuating the covenant. — Allen Ross and

John N. Oswalt, Cornerstone Biblical Commentary: Genesis, Exodus, vol. 1 (Carol Stream, IL: Tyndale House Publishers, 2008), 149.

4. Verse 3. What is the lesson for parents?

My Christian friend, if you have a boy or girl in your home who is marriageable, you ought to pray that he will not marry one of the "Canaanites". They are still in the land, and there is always a danger of our young people marrying one of them. If they do, as someone has put it, they are going to have the devil for their father-in-law, and they are always going to have trouble with him. —J. Vernon McGee, *Thru the Bible Commentary, electronic ed., vol.* 1 (Nashville: Thomas Nelson, 1997), 98.

5. 2 Corinthians 6.14 spells out what Genesis 24 implies. How would you paraphrase this verse?

Some people are trying to live in two worlds. They want to walk in the light on Sunday and live in darkness the other six days of the week. But they need to decide. The devil loves darkness. It's worth noting that a lot of crimes are committed at night. Hell is described as outer darkness. Darkness is the devil's domain.

But God lives in the light. That is why Scripture tells us to wake up from our sleep and cast off the works of darkness. Ephesians 5:8 says, "For though your hearts were once full of darkness, now you are full of light from the Lord, and your behavior should show it!" (NLT).

That is why the Bible says, "Don't team up with those who are unbelievers. How can goodness be a partner with wickedness? How can light live with darkness?" (2 Cor. 6:14 NLT). This doesn't mean that Christians can't have friends or associates who are not Christians. The Bible is speaking here of being yoked together in a close union where you are walking with someone.

The Bible says you can't live in two worlds. If you are going to be a true Christian, then there will be things you have to say no to. You will have to decide.

Have you been trying to live in darkness? It is hard to hide light, because it leaks out. A little light can go a long way. We need to let our lights shine before others—not try to hide our light or hide our Christianity. Let's hold it up for all to see. — Greg Laurie, *For Every Season, Volume Two* (Dana Point, CA: Kerygma Publishing—Allen David Books, 2011).

6. Genesis 24.7. What do we learn about following God from Abraham's example in this verse?

Abraham is really a man of faith. He demonstrates it again and again, and here he is magnificent. He says to this servant, "You can count on God to lead you. God has promised me this." Abraham is not taking a leap in the dark—faith is not a leap in the dark. It must rest upon the Word of God. Many people say, "I believe God, and it will come to pass." That's fine. It is wonderful for you to believe God, but do you have something in writing from Him? Abraham always asked for it in writing, and he had it in writing from God. God had made a contract with him. Abraham is really saying, "God has promised me that through my seed Isaac He is going to bring a blessing to the world. You can be sure of one thing: God has a bride back there for Isaac." You see, Abraham rests upon what God has said. We need to not be foolish today. Faith is not foolishness. It is resting upon something. It is always reasonable. It is never a leap in the dark. It is not betting your life that this or that will come to pass. It is not a gamble; it is a sure thing. Faith is the real sure thing. Abraham is sure. — J. Vernon McGee, *Thru the Bible Commentary, electronic ed., vol. 1* (Nashville: Thomas Nelson, 1997), 98.

7. Verse 8. Why wasn't Isaac to go back with the servant? You would think he would want to go and help pick out his own wife.

Furthermore, the refusal is repeated once more in v. 8, leaving an indelible impression in the reader's mind that Isaac must under no circumstances leave Canaan. The reason for this insistence that Isaac stay in Canaan is that the offspring of Abraham and the land of Canaan together symbolize the early stages of the fulfillment of God's promises. As Van Seters observes,

> It is precisely in v. 7a that we are given the reason why Isaac is not to return to Abraham's homeland. It is because God took him from there to give, under oath, this new land to his offspring, and, therefore, for Isaac to return to his father's homeland would be a rejection of that promise.

At the same time, the insistence that Isaac should not return seems strange in the light of Jacob's later return to the same place. Isaac is also warned not to go to Egypt during a famine. Abraham went to Egypt and Jacob to both Haran and Egypt, but Isaac never leaves Canaan. — James McKeown, *Genesis, The Two Horizons Old Testament Commentary* (Grand Rapids, MI; Cambridge, U.K.: William B. Eerdmans Publishing Company, 2008), 122.

8. What do these ten camels suggest about Abraham?

Today we associate camels with the Middle East, but domesticated camels were not common during Abraham's time. Since they were rare and made ideal pack animals for long journeys, each beast represented a small fortune. Ten camels in Abraham's day would have looked like a ten-limousine entourage today. After nearly a month long journey, the servant arrived in a region in northern Mesopotamia known as Aram-naharaim, which means Aram of the Two Rivers, bounded by the great rivers Tigris and Euphrates. — Charles R. Swindoll, *Abraham: One Nomad's Amazing Journey of Faith* (Carol Stream, IL: Tyndale, 2014).

9. Is there any correlation between being wealthy and being godly?

The Bible teaches that wealth is of medium importance. Abraham was wealthy and it is, generally speaking, good to be wealthy. Just, don't want wealth too much.

One of the hardest things to describe is medium. It is easy to talk about something that is really big or really small, a movie that is really funny or really sad. It is more difficult to describe medium. Wealth's importance could best be described as medium.

Wealth is not as important as your integrity. It is not as important as your relationships. It is not so important that it makes sense to work 60 hours a week and never see your wife and kids. No one ever lies on the death bed and says, "I wish I had spent more time at the office making money."

On the other hand, if you can make more money, do so. It affords you some margin to take your wife out on a nice date night or a nice vacation. It may mean memories at Disneyland with your kids. It may mean you can support a myriad of worthy causes.

Wealth is of some importance, but not too much. I would describe its importance as medium. — Josh Hunt, *Following God* (Pulpit Press, 2014).

10. Genesis 24.12. Is praying for success part of your regular prayer life? Should it be?

I remember hearing a friend say he was preaching a series of sermons on success. My first thought was, "how worldly."

I don't remember any other sermons I have heard on success.

Success is a popular topic in the world, but not too popular in the church. It is mentioned quite a bit in the Bible. Here are a few examples:

- Then he prayed, "LORD, God of my master Abraham, make me successful today, and show kindness to my master Abraham. Genesis 24:12

- In everything he did he had great success, because the LORD was with him. 1 Samuel 18:14

- Keep this Book of the Law always on your lips; meditate on it day and night, so that you may be careful to do everything written in it. Then you will be prosperous and successful. Joshua 1:8

- LORD, save us! LORD, grant us success! Psalm 118:25
- He holds success in store for the upright, He is a shield to those whose walk is blameless, Proverbs 2:7

Are you hesitant to pray, "Lord, grant me success today!" Don't be. Pray for God's success as you work for Him. — Josh Hunt, *Following God* (Pulpit Press, 2014).

11. Genesis 12.14. As we seek to follow the will of God, do you think we should lay out specific tests like this one—"If she offers to give my camels something to drink, I know she is the one."

Here's a second guideline: Saturate the entire process in prayer.

That said, I don't recommend laying out specific tests or parameters for the Lord. Don't say, "If she shows up to the blind date wearing a sweater with red in it, I'll take it from You, Lord, that she's the one I am to marry." That's not how God works today. Eliezer didn't have the advantages of Scripture to read or the inward leading of the Holy Spirit. He did, however, have Abraham's promise that God would provide supernatural leading.

Also notice that the servant's parameters weren't random or arbitrary. He looked for the woman who demonstrated uncommon hospitality. Drawing and lugging water required hard work. In the evening, the women came out to the spring with clay jars to fill and carry home—a tiring chore all by itself. He presumed to add to their work by asking for a drink for himself. — Charles R. Swindoll, *Abraham: One Nomad's Amazing Journey of Faith* (Carol Stream, IL: Tyndale, 2014).

12. This is an example of "putting out a fleece." Where does that phrase come from? Should we put out a fleece?

In His providence, God brought Rebekah to the well just as the servant was praying; and she did exactly what the servant had been praying about. The servant did what Gideon would do years later, "put out a fleece" (Jud. 6:36–40). This is not the best way for God's people to determine the will of God, because the conditions we lay down for God to meet might not be in His will. We are walking by sight and not by faith, and we may end up tempting God. However, God accommodated Himself to the needs of the servant (and Gideon) and guided them as they requested. — Warren W. Wiersbe, *Be Obedient, "Be" Commentary Series* (Wheaton, IL: Victor Books, 1991), 119.

13. God apparently had Rebekah picked out for Isaac. Does God have one special person picked out for us?

You're right that we've made it a point in many Boundless articles to urge people to stop looking for "the one," to think biblically about whom they choose to marry, and to stop asking, "Is he right (for me)?" All of these exhortations grow out of our concern with the trend to search endlessly for the perfect match, as if doing all that work before marriage will ensure smooth sailing after the wedding. There are many dangers to thinking this way, not least of which is concluding — once the bumps in the road appear, and they always do (1 Corinthians 7:28) — that you married the wrong one.

As I've written before, once you're married, that is the right one. Biblical marriage is permanent (Matthew 19:6).

This doesn't mean, however, that God doesn't know in advance who we will marry. Should you marry, God will have been the one who brought your husband to you. Even our wedding vows affirm this: "What God has joined together, let man not separate." He is Sovereign over all that He has made. But it is also true that we are free to choose whom we will marry. God made us stewards of all that He has made and has given us the opportunity to think and choose free from coercion. We are responsible (2 Corinthians 5:10, Ezekiel 18:20, Galatians 6:8). Though these ideas seem in tension, they are not mutually exclusive. And that tension — God's sovereignty and our responsibility — runs throughout Scripture.

http://www.boundless.org/advice/2014/is-god-sovereign-over-whom-i-marry

14. Verse 12. What do we learn about following God from this servant's example?

If the first important feature of this passage is relationships, the second is prayer. This great servant of Abraham had never read 1 Thessalonians 5:17 ("pray continually"). It was not written until two thousand years later. But this man understood the principle of prevailing prayer and faithfully practiced what he understood. Was ever an expedition more constantly bathed in prayer than this one? We are not told specifically of all the prayers the servant uttered on his way out and back from Nahor, but if the immediacy and fervency of the recorded prayer is any indication, each step of the journey must have been marked by a fervent seeking of God's direction and blessing. I would not doubt that the caravan began each day's march with prayer that God would prosper it, keep it from harm, and bring it to the place where its mission could be most quickly fulfilled. No doubt the days also ended with prayer as this great servant thanked God that he was now closer to the realization of his goal.

Yet as he prayed, he kept traveling—and he must have kept planning how he would proceed once he got to his appointed destination. This means that prayer is no substitute for action. This servant prayed and worked at the same time, for he knew that prayer is given not to make work unnecessary but to make it effective. — *An Expositional Commentary – Genesis, Volume 2: A New Beginning (Genesis 12-36).*

15. Verse 15. How long did it take God to answer this prayer?

Every godly prayer is answered before the prayer itself is finished—"Before he had finished praying..." This is because Christ has pledged in His Word, "My Father will give you whatever you ask in my name" (John 16:23). When you ask in faith and in Christ's name—that is, in oneness with Him and His will—"it will be given to you" (John 15:7).

Since God's Word cannot fail, whenever we meet this simple condition, the answer to our prayer has already been granted and is complete in heaven as we pray, even though it may not be revealed on earth until much later. Therefore it is wise to close every prayer with praise to God for the answer He has already given. —L. B. COWMAN, from Streams in the Desert / Thomas Nelson, *A Daybook of Prayer: Meditations, Scriptures and Prayers to Draw near to the Heart of God* (Nashville: Thomas Nelson, 2006).

16. Genesis 24.19. How big of a deal was it to give these camels something to drink?

What do you look for in a wife, a friend or business partner? One answer to this question might be the little French word: Lagniappe. It means, "a little extra."

You want someone who will do a little extra. You want someone who will go beyond the call of duty. You want someone who will do more than is required.

This is what Abraham's servant found in Rebekah, "I'll draw water for your camels too, until they have had enough to drink." Genesis 24:19

This was no small feat. I read one commentary that suggested there would likely have been ten camels and each camel can drink twenty gallons of water. This may have taken her an hour.

This is the kind of person I want to be, how about you? I want to be a person who says, "Let me get some water for your camels too."

My sister does consulting for spas. I can reduce the advice she gives to clients to one phrase: surprise and delight. It is good business. It is what Rebekah did. — Josh Hunt, *Following God* (Pulpit Press, 2014).

17. What does this tell you about Rebekah?

Where does wealth come from? Hard work. How does a whole nation become wealthy? Hard work.

- Hard work always pays off; mere talk puts no bread on the table. Proverbs 14:23 (The Message)

- Indolence wants it all and gets nothing; the energetic have something to show for their lives. Proverbs 13:4 (The Message)

- The diligent find freedom in their work; the lazy are oppressed by work. Proverbs 12:24 (The Message)

Rebekah didn't mind working hard, as Swindoll explains:

> Most anyone would offer a sip to a thirsty stranger. Watering ten camels, on the other hand, took a lot of extra effort—especially considering that each camel could drink as much as fifty gallons in three minutes. And he had ten thirsty animals! A five-gallon jar weighed almost fifty pounds. For a woman to volunteer to water someone's camels would mean offering to haul five hundred gallons, five gallons at a time. (Don't worry, I'll do the math.) That's one hundred trips back and forth from the spring. (Bear with me a little further.) If each trip took only a minute, she just added two hours of backbreaking work to her already busy day. — Josh Hunt, *Following God* (Pulpit Press, 2014).

18. Could Rebekah have known how important her actions were?

Little did Rebekah know that doing a humble task for a stranger would make her the bride of a wealthy man who was in a covenant relationship with God. She would become the mother of Jacob, and he would become the father of the twelve tribes of Israel! Years ago, I read a quotation from a writer identified only as "Marsden," and it has stuck with me: "Make every occasion a great occasion, for you can never tell when someone may be taking your measure for a larger place." — Warren W. Wiersbe, *Be Obedient, "Be" Commentary* Series (Wheaton, IL: Victor Books, 1991), 119–120.

19. What do you want to recall from today's study?

20. How can we support one another in prayer this week?

Made in the USA
Coppell, TX
30 December 2024